The Buddha in Hell
and Other Alarms

The Buddha in Hell
and Other Alarms

Distressing Near-Death Experiences
in Perspective

Nancy Evans Bush

ISBN 978-0-9851917-1-9

Paperback by IngramSpark, contains a bibliography and index.

Cover by Susan Pomeroy, The Web Geographer

Cover photograph: Close-up of the Helix Nebula. NASA, NOAO, ESA, the Hubble Helix Nebula Team, M.Meixner (STScl) and T.A. Rector (NRAO)

Internal design by WordZWorth, Ltd.

Index by Carol Roberts

Contact: *http://www.dancingpastthedark.com*

CONTENTS

"Be patient toward all that is unsolved in your heart and try to love the questions themselves... Do not seek the answers, which cannot be given you because you would not be able to live them. And the point is to live everything. Live the questions now. Perhaps you will then gradually, without noticing it, live along some distant day into the answer."

—RAINER MARIA RILKE,
FROM *LETTERS TO A YOUNG POET*

PREFACE

NOTE: This book is not a collection of first-person accounts of distressing NDEs. Those are widely available online on sites such as iands.org, ndestories.org, and near-death.com, to name only three. Also, my previous book, *Dancing Past the Dark*, a reader-friendly, research-based introduction to the subject, includes a small collection of accounts of distressing experiences. This book invites reflection on how we interpret disturbing near-death and similar experiences, especially those which may be understood as suggesting hell.

HEAVEN

When news of heaven arrived late in the twentieth century, it caused a sensation. Bookstores and news programs overflowed with the stories of men and women who said they had been clinically dead—or perhaps seriously ill, or in an accident or other life-threatening situation—when something happened. (They said, "You'll probably think I'm crazy, but...")

They had found themselves alert and going somewhere, some of them able to look back and see their body lying where it had been left, then seeing wonderful light or beautiful landscapes, being greeted joyfully by people they loved who had died, often feeling surrounded by perfect love. Surely this sounded like heaven! The men and women, all of them deeply affected, said it felt 'realer than real,' and they would never fear death again.

The events were called near-death experiences (abbreviated as 'NDEs'), and suddenly dying sounded less fearful, even welcoming. Skeptics claimed they were hoaxes or hallucinations. Enthusiasts said they were proof of an afterlife. At least one physician called them "Bunk, hokum, and poppycock!" And a few pioneering physicians and psychologists risked their careers by studying them and publishing the first research results.

No one was quite certain how to understand the NDEs, but clearly there were a lot of them, and they changed people's lives.

In those early years, I was hired to tend the office of the fledgling International Association for Near-Death Studies, housed at the University of Connecticut. Soon I was among the handful of speakers trying to answer questions from entranced audiences wanting to know, "What is it like to die?"

I remember vividly how utterly still those audiences were. Death had historically been presented as a terrifying prospect— grinning skeletons at Hallowe'en, the hooded Grim Reaper with his scythe—but now here were these beautiful stories of light and an all-encompassing love, of fearlessness and wanting to stay in the NDE rather than coming back to ordinary life. Could it be true?

The hope, the prayerfulness in the listening of those audiences was like a presence, it was so strong. And almost always there was a moment when a braver-than-usual person asked cautiously: "I wonder…is there…you know…is there the other kind of experience?" And the audience held its breath.

No one was certain, in those early days, just how to answer. There was a lot of evasion. More than anyone else on those speaking engagements, I knew there was another kind of experience, that not all NDEs were reassuring.

Twenty years earlier, during the delivery of my second baby, there had been what I thought of as The Dream, though it was realer than any dream. (The term 'near-death experience' had not yet been invented.), I had found myself abruptly outside the hospital, flying. I could see the school where I taught, and from that concluded that the large metal boxes below me were on the hospital roof; but then I was leaving, moving into deep space. After a while of traveling, I was taunted by a group of authoritative circle-like figures with the message that I was not real, had never been real, that I had only been allowed to imagine my life. Earth, they announced, was an illusion, and so were my baby, the toddler at home, my mom, my husband, everyone I thought I knew. There was no home to go back to. Not only I but humanity itself was not real. And then the circles moved off, and the 'I' which seemed to be nothing but consciousness was left alone in an empty universe, wracked by a shocked grief which seemed all too real.

For a young woman who knew almost nothing about metaphysics or Eastern philosophies—who was, in fact, thoroughly mainstream-American, liberal Creation-based, evolution-believing, incarnational, social justice Protestant—it was a horrific experience, and for twenty years it had haunted my thinking, my religious life, my everyday expectations, my understanding of the world. I had never spoken about it, not to anyone. It was too much to put into words.

Despite that experience, I still did not know what to say to those audiences more than thirty-five years ago. This book is about what I wish I could have said to them. (I do hope some have found their way to my first book, *Dancing Past the Dark*, and to the blog.)

What we know now

We know now that although the great majority of near-death experiences are beautiful beyond description, some are not. For almost one in five people who have an NDE, the memory may be traumatic.

How are we to understand such things? Our common explanations come from the medieval Christian view of hell as eternal torment, or perhaps from the Law of Attraction which says "they brought it on themselves," or from theories of psychosis, or simply dismissal as hallucinations and fairy tales.

My premise, always, finds its image in photographs from the Hubble telescope. We are part of a dynamic universe which operates in an unceasing flow of radiance and darkness, violence and entropy, wholeness and fragmentation, the explosive glory of dying novas and the implacable pull of black holes that may give birth to baby universes.

Our experiences, all of them, inhabit and are governed and interpreted within this same universe. Just as darkness is real but not the only reality in the universe, it is not conclusive in these experiences, either; so the surest foundation for understanding a deeply disturbing near-death experience is to learn as much as possible about all sorts of NDEs. Some are perceived as the heights of spiritual experience; others—those this book is about—represent the depths. All lie within the mystery that is Being itself. There is more about the nature of the universe and our own consciousness than what we know, and more even than our religions and philosophies and sciences can tell us.

Other than the experience of a Burmese monk, the focus of this book is not on first-person accounts of distressing NDEs, or on research. (The book *Dancing Past the Dark*, which serves as a research-based primer on the subject, offers a collection of the accounts; they are also widely available online on sites such as iands.org, ndestories.org, near-death.com). The essays here are conversational, written more to reflect on how we think about them and less to offer research results data about dNDEs. Here the focus is on psychological, philosophical, and spiritual aspects of the experiences.

Much of the material here began as blog posts or conference presentations or articles first published elsewhere; it has all been edited or rewritten for this book. A couple of chapters come by the gracious permission of other authors. If you have questions or observations about anything you read here, you are invited to join the conversation in the comments section of the blog, *http:// www.dancingpastthedark.com*.

Nancy Evans Bush
Oak Island, North Carolina, June 2016

PART I

NEAR-DEATH EXPERIENCE

CHAPTER 1

The Buddha in Hell Redux

A flurry of agitation accompanied the Internet news that a former Buddhist monk in Myanmar (Burma) was claiming that in his near-death experience he had seen the Buddha in hell. He said Yama, king of the Buddhist hells, had shown him a terrible lake of fire which held not only the Buddha but famous spiritual and political figures much-loved throughout the country. Goliath was in the lake, too, the giant from the Bible. They were there, he said Yama told him, because they did not believe in the Christian God. They did not accept Jesus.

The experience was so stunning, the monk was converted instantly. Although he claimed to have had no prior exposure to Christianity, he no sooner woke up than he began preaching, going from church to church selling audiotapes about his experience. Reactions varied, of course, from acceptance by those Christians who believed his account to be literally true, to rejection by Christians who flatly did not believe it, to resentment and disbelief from his former Buddhist community.

But the Buddha in hell! What are we to make of this? Was he really in hell? Does this mean that Christianity is more true than Buddhism? And if the monk saw a lake of fire, doesn't that prove that hell is a real place? Well, no...sigh...it doesn't actually prove any of that. But it does prove how powerful a strong NDE can be.

I looked up the account on Google, and sure enough, there it was, and still is. The story was Big News, though the account was several years old. Actually, there are different versions (which is a clue that wariness will be appropriate). Nevertheless, it's a fascinating story. You can do an internet search for it or copy this into your search box: *http://amightywind.com/whatsnew/071112buddhist.htm*

Over the course of a few days I heard from several people breathless with excitement about the story, so I posted something about it on the *dancingpastthedark* blog (Bush, 2012). What interests me as much as the story itself is that in the four years since then, that post has had hundreds of hits. It is consistently the blog's most-requested post. Why?

The post I wrote was hastily done, a knee-jerk response to an NDE account I saw as far likelier to be a case of missionary manipulation than theological revelation. It was not only skeptical but superficial, and has needed revisiting. So here we are...the Buddha in Hell Redux.

THE MONK'S STORY

If you have read the account (which I recommend), you know that a man who gives his name as Athet Pyan Shinthaw Paulu presents what sounds like a believable autobiographical background of his life in Myanmar, how he was raised and came to be living as a monk. It sounds credible, even down to details like the sea crocodile that destroyed his boat. (I looked it up—and yes, there are such crocodiles in that area, and that is the kind of behavior one would expect of them.)

The account tells how he came to enter training to be a monk and describes his respect for his teacher. He says he became a monk and was renamed U Nata Pannita Ashinthuriya. Then he says he lived for quite a few years devoted to his spiritual practice and to the principles of Buddhism.

So far, so good. It's clear and it seems (at least to a Western reader) to be credible. The monk reports that he was so scrupulous he refused even to harm a mosquito that might infect him with malaria, which one did, and it turned out to be the disease that nearly killed him. Actually, his account claims that he had both malaria and yellow fever.

The monk continues, "I learned later that I actually died for three days. My body decayed and stunk of death, and my heart stopped beating."

And then comes his NDE, in which the terrifying deity Yama, king of the Buddhist hells, escorts the monk through a very Christian description of hell, giving Christian reasons why it is occupied by so many Buddhist luminaries who led exemplary lives. I am not going to fall into the pit I did with my first commentary, which was (how could I?) to quibble about the content of his NDE. Read it, or listen to it on YouTube.

The monk awakened, he says, on his funeral pyre, in the presence of his parents and many witnesses. When he climbed out of his coffin the crowd scattered in terror, but he began immediately to tell of his experience, the debut of his quite literal revivalist ministry.

> I told them about the men I had seen in the lake of fire, and...that our forefathers and us [sic] have been deceived for thousands of years! I told them everything we believe is a lie.

Such has been the power of his testimony, he says, that his story shocked the whole region, and more than three hundred monks became Christians and started to read the Bible. (He has also said it was seven thousand monks who converted.) The former monk, now called Paul, appears to have supported himself for some time by distributing tapes of his experience and speaking to churches and house groups.

SUSPICIONS

It is all too easy, with such a multi-layered experience account, to dismiss it out of hand as outlandish, which is what I did in my first response to the story. A more careful reading brings up deeper and more important issues.

Skepticism about factual errors and autobiographical truthfulness compound doubts about controversial NDE content. Some statements appear to have been added by someone who does not know Burma, as with the claim that the monk had both malaria and yellow fever. But yellow fever is a disease of some parts of South America and Africa; in fact, the Centers for Disease Control states explicitly, "There is no yellow fever in Burma." What else, then, may be untrue?

Is it true that his body was actually decaying when he revived, or is this for dramatic effect?

A number of issues are plain to Burmese eyes but invisible to most Westerners, such as the observation that a novice monk's new name would begin with 'shin,' never with the 'U' he claims. Or that he said he became a monk at 19, though the entry age for becoming a fully ordained monk is 20. Or that the monk's "claim to have seen Aung San, the revolutionary leader of Myanmar (father of opposition leader, Aung San Suu Kyi) in hell *'because he persecuted and killed Christians, but mostly because he didn't believe in Jesus Christ'* was completely without foundation. Aung San is a well-known figure in Burmese/Myanmar thinking and history - and there is no evidence at all that he persecuted any Christians, let alone killed any."

Most troubling to that commenter is the monk's statement that his teacher died in a car crash in 1983. In fact, his teacher died in 1977, making it doubtful that the monk could have studied under him. ("The Hoax Story of Remarkable Testimony of a Buddhist Monk in Myanmar Burma Who Came Back to Life.")

A Buddhist reader noted, "With due respect, this is not even a proper Christian message. It is just scare tactics." *http://www. dorjeshugden.com/forum/index.php?topic=2211.0*

Several commenters have noted that, had the story been true, that three hundred Buddhist monks converted to Christianity—and especially if there were as many as seven *thousand*—the news would have spread rapidly beyond any effort of the government-controlled media to suppress it.

We are left wondering, who is this monk, this Athet Pyan Shinthaw Paulu behind so much story-telling and factual distortion? One source says that "A number of people in Myanmar who personally know him, or have met him, believe he is in need of medical help and counselling." *http://etb-pseudoscience.blogspot. com/2012/04/christians-debunk-resurrection-of.html*

The thicket of gossip, rumors, and scandal has led to claims that "It is now a serious crime to listen to the tapes, because the government wants to dampen the sensation."

The rumors and scandal are all yours on Google.

THOUGHTS

What is *not* on that Google site is any discussion about the nature of such experiences and how to interpret them. The images of many experiences are powerful and haunting, and often literally persuasive; but they come, most unfortunately, with no guidelines to interpret their coding. In this case, considerable evidence suggests that we discount the monk's story for factual inaccuracies; but there is still that strong central imagery with its cognitive dissonance. If we look beyond the religious tract language and the farcical elements of the deeply Buddhist Yama appearing as a proselytizing guide to a Christian hell, beyond the gossip and rumors of mental illness, there may be clues to what is really going on. Looking more deeply brings up the underlying story as *a classic instance of a life-shattering near-death experience which throws everybody off by its spectacular implausibility.*

What I already knew at some level but had been ignoring was that the kinds of details which seem most ludicrous to us as onlookers are likely to be the most important and disruptive for the experiencer. I had not looked through the monk's lens.

Try this for cognitive dissonance: Think about your own deepest faith, whether it's a religion or an ideology (atheism, materialism, Marxism, etc.)—however you explain how the world really works. Next, imagine yourself in this monk's position. You find yourself in the worst nightmare you've ever had, bigger, crazier, darker, one that is realer than your everyday waking reality; it is so real, it is beyond arguing.

Toward you comes a visible, larger-than-life entity of immense authority. This is *his territory*, and he towers over you with utterly unquestionable power. He pulls you with him toward a horrid scene: a lake full of fire, and out there, burning, people you recognize, whether living or dead, people you trust, people you follow. They are the ones who have helped you define your world. Why are they out there in this fire? Because, this supernatural being who really knows tells you, *they believed the wrong things! They told you the wrong things!* And this means that *you believe the wrong things, too!* It could be *you, burning in that lake of fire!* And his power and his knowing are so great, you suddenly understand: It's true: *You know nothing true. Everything you believe is a lie!* As you stand there, every certainty you have about the world falls away. Your lifetime of faith is pulled apart.

Psychotherapist John Ryan Haule has written about confronting this kind of shock:

"[It] is to be exposed to the unthinkable. The world cannot be as I have constructed it; it is unimaginably different. It constitutes the death of everything I have come to know and depend upon. I am not who I thought I was and the world is not as I assembled it" (1999).

And then there is my favorite quote about this existential shock, from psychotherapist and near-death experiencer Alex

Lukeman. He has called the shock of recognizing a different reality "...the ego's encounter with the underlying unconscious and transcendent dynamics of the [Holy]." He describes it as "destruction of traditional and habitual patterns of perception and understanding, including religious belief structures and socially accepted concepts of the nature of human existence and behavior" (1998).

And that is what happened to the monk. And what could happen to any of us having a similar experience. This particular example includes cross-cultural imagery, which is not uncommon in NDEs, including very strongly in my own experience. With or without the cross-cultural element, these happenings certainly can insert new ideas or raise doctrinal questions, creating bewilderment and spiritual havoc.

For an outsider, it very likely seems amusing, maybe even hilarious, to hear that a deity of one religion is unapologetically proselytizing for another religion. It seems a clear tip-off to the narrator's naïveté and sermonizing intention. But what if the observer is not an outsider but a devout Buddhist, an unsophisticated and perhaps emotionally fragile monk who is actually experiencing the destruction of his "traditional and habitual patterns of perception and understanding, including religious belief structures and socially accepted concepts of the nature of human existence"?

If we have paid attention to all the literature about strongly compelling spiritual experiences, or have listened to people we know who have had a deep NDE, it will be obvious that such intensity could indeed turn the monk's life around on the Burmese equivalent of a dime. We have heard others with that same intensity, that same drive to tell *everyone* the compelling truth of an overwhelming message.

To believe the account as literally true is farcical; to experience it spiritually could be cataclysmic. That is the point I had overlooked entirely in my original post. During a re-reading of my files about the monk's account, several phrases practically jumped from the page:

I immediately started to explain the things I had seen and heard. People were astonished. I told them about the men I had seen in the lake of fire, and... *that our forefathers and us have been deceived for thousands of years! I told them everything we believe is a lie.*

From the Epilogue of this version of the story, a spokesperson for a Christian oversight group comments: (Babinski)

Since 'Paul who came back to life' experienced the above story *he has remained a faithful witness... His testimony is obviously very uncompromising.* Because of that, his message has offended many people...Despite great opposition, *his experiences were so real to him that he has not wavered.* [Emphasis added.]

The point is that just like countless other NDErs, 'Paul' accepted the immediate perceptual level of his experience as being total truth. That is the power of this kind of archetypal event, that to the individual involved, it feels unquestionably real and unshakably true in a material sense. He does not think to take it apart and examine the pieces, nor to wonder about alternative meanings. Who is present to say that, in actuality, the imagery will feel truer and be easier to deal with if it is treated as symbolic? Usually, no one.

What is the emotional impact? His sense of reality has been shattered. The new perception is that the world is not as he believed it to be. "We have been deceived for thousands of years... everything we [*meaning, 'we Buddhists'*] believe is a lie!"

"Despite great opposition...he has not wavered."

How are we to understand all this? There is now abundant data that experiences like this are not simply hallucinations; brain scans register them differently, and people recall them differently. They carry sometimes life-changing meanings for the people who have them; yet it is often a mistake to interpret them literally. Neither are they deliberately imaginative products; no one consciously constructs the inside of a near-death or similar experience. How are we to make sense of them?

Neither of the Internet accounts of the monk's experience (I have read both) sounds entirely genuine. Unknown editorial hands have obviously been at work, whether of non-Burmese missionaries inadvertently inserting factual errors, or of the monk himself, hoping to build dramatic effect (an already-decaying body, numberless converting monks). As the many online comments show, its evangelical appeal is limited; mainstream churches declined to hear him, there is no record of a swell of Buddhist monks converting, and eventually his audience dwindled to small Pentecostal groups.

I wrote earlier of my belief that either the account is a flat-out Christian testimonial that has been entirely faked, or it originated in an actual Burmese near-death experience which was then heavily edited at the hand of a Christian evangelical interpreter. I now suspect that much of that interpretation may have come from the monk himself as he increased his contacts with the missionary community and his fluency with evangelical language. But I have come to believe, contrary to my first, altogether Western view, that behind this spectacular, flawed, and bogus-sounding NDE account there is a very real Something which happened to a confused Burmese monk who has given us the only interpretation he knew.

What I am now seeing is a strong similarity to the situation of the young Alex Malarkey, of *The Boy Who Came Back from Heaven*. There is no reason to doubt that as a small child he had a near-death experience with elements of an encounter which he described as being in heaven. For Alex, his experience became cripplingly distorted because its content did not jibe with the inflexible biblical expectations of his mother. With no one to help him integrate the NDE with scripture, and in a blitz of suffocating media attention on one hand and fundamentalist demands on the other, he was eventually compelled to disown the experience entirely. He is left with the charge that he had perpetrated a hoax.

The monk, also rudderless, salvaged what he could. Both he and Alex have adapted to fit the fundamentalist mold. Nevertheless, he remains an outsider to both the Buddhist community which was his origin and the majority of the Christian community which does not deal easily with encounters with a hell. In his frustration I am remembering the voices of others...a Lutheran pastor's wife, frantic because no one would believe she knew how to bring world peace but whose family members, their car running, gathered outside her barricaded door to take her to the psychiatric hospital; the Canadian man driven to tell everyone, endlessly, about his vision which verified to him the eternal priesthood of Melchizedek; the young suburban mother who could not, would not stop telling the world about her experience in heaven. So how *are* we to understand such experiences?

LAST WORDS REDUX

Two things I believe are really important when trying to understand what any spiritual experience means: 1) Like dreams, visionary experiences carry their messages in symbol, not in the observable, fact-filled terms of everyday speech. Taking them as their literal representation is rarely accurate. 2) In much the same way, near-death experiences seem directed to universal elements of the human spirit and psychology generally; as experiences, they do not customarily carry doctrinal messages for specific religions, although we often interpret them afterwards in terms of the traditions we know.

I don't scoff at cross-cultural content, because my NDE included figures which I later learned were the Chinese Yin/Yang symbol. It was not until I discovered, years after the NDE, the significance of the Yin/Yang, that I could interpret the experience adequately as an intensely personal event. I now know that the presence of the symbol in my experience was not to say that Buddhism is right and Christianity wrong. It took a very long time for me to understand that neither the Yin/Yang nor the experience itself was delivering a teaching about religious doctrine but was functioning as a symbol of something else entirely—like an arrow pointing beyond itself.

We see fire in an experience like the monk's and immediately, culturally, think "punishment in eternal torment." However, fire has traditionally been associated with the presence of God, as with Moses and the burning bush. In fact, the Bible includes some ninety references to the presence of God as fire. Suppose the monk's NDE were interpreted as seeing the Buddha and wise men immersed in holiness? We can do the same with any element of a spiritual experience—ask what might it mean, other than what seems to be sitting right on the surface. Are there other ways of interpreting the monk's NDE, beyond the physically literal? Of course. Did the monk have access to those ways of thinking? Quite possibly not. Had he been encouraged to be patient with interpreting his experience, and to go sit quietly, and turn it over in his mind, and think what else it might be saying—who knows what he might have discovered!

We can look at these troubling experience accounts and recoil, choosing to interpret them as pointing to the traditional, literal, punitive hell. But that is our choice. We can also choose to take the time and trouble to explore what else they might mean, what they may be pointing to about our lives or our way of thinking that could use some change, or that would revolutionize our approach to life itself.

Yes, it is now clear that there are some really scary spiritual experiences. Having worked my way through one, I know just how cataclysmic they can feel. But am I ready, after all these years, to say they point to a concept like a condemnatory hell? Not on your life. Or mine, either. The same universe, the same God, that has room for these profoundly traumatic events also brings the glorious and/or peaceful spiritual experiences, the ones people believe indicate heaven. In something of the same way, Hubble photos show us wonderful, serene visions of "what's out there" along with black holes and incomprehensible violence. Why should our spiritual landscape be different than that of the universe we inhabit? We are required to learn how to be with it all, in ways that make sense to us.

What does not make sense to many people today is the notion of a physical place in which the errors of a brief human life will be punished with great cruelty forever. As one letter-writer wonderfully put it to me, it makes no sense that a God of this vast universe would display such wrath toward two small creatures simply because they "ate fruit and had opinions." We can rethink hell without diminishing its power.

I have come to believe that the NDE which at first seemed to destroy my faith has turned out to be a dubious gift but a gift nonetheless, simply because it has required me to examine these kinds of questions with such care. I hope the monk's experience has proven similar for him. As the well-known experiencer Howard Storm could tell him, countless individuals over history have endured a shamanic initiation experience which stripped them painfully of one existence and exchanged it for one more satisfying. Who's to say that was punishment?

CHAPTER 2

On the Wholeness of Darkness and Light

*The greatest question facing humankind is,
'Is the universe friendly?'*

—ALBERT EINSTEIN

A woman has written to say that she heard about distressing near-death experiences at a conference of the International Association for Near Death Studies (IANDS). "It sounded weird," she said. "Are these just nightmares?"

Well, all near-death experiences appear to share something of the same space as the dream world, and no doubt they do sound weird. But then, when looked at from the perspective of everyday consciousness, just about everything in this field of near-death studies sounds weird, at least at first.

It has been forty years since Raymond Moody's book *Life After Life* presented his collection of accounts of consciousness at the edge of death, the narratives he named "near-death experiences." Weird or not, it is clear that he touched a nerve that still quivers.

THE NERVE OF MORTALITY

Actually, the nerve of mortality has always quivered in creatures with consciousness. We see it in photographs of apes and elephants grieving the loss of one of their own, of crows mourning, and loyal pets refusing to leave the grave of their owner; we see it in the personal jewelry and objects found in the graves of our earliest ancestors, buried tens of thousands of years before us, clues that they also wondered, "What does it mean that we become not-alive? Where do we go?"

In the earliest written language, we hear their questions woven into metaphors of darkness and light, death and rebirth. Across thousands of years, we can still dimly see that they understood their non-physical experiences as a part of reality, and that, like us, they longed for reassurance. The sum total of their human experience was held in paintings and intricate metalwork, and in dances and poems and stories, like baskets in which to carry their meanings. Their images and words are the raw materials from which have come our myth and religion, the deep cultural assumptions which hold us even today.

Today we know more about the physical structures of life than they did; but they were more open to its invisible, imaginative depths. It has become a cliché to say that in some ways the scientific Enlightenment has closed down our understandings, as over the past four hundred years quantitative method and rational skepticism have led us to prefer the literal meanings of numbers, not poetry; of psychology, not religion. Compared with our ancestors, we are uncomfortable with metaphor and disdainful of myth, enamored of data and dismissive of symbol.

Moody's revelation of near-death experience was not presented in terms of religion, which by the twentieth century had distanced itself from the sciences. No, the subject as he presented it was *consciousness*. That made the subject approachable by almost everyone. And as proof is our bedrock of believability, Moody's findings gave something to everyone: some took them as proof of life after death but virtually everyone, religious or not, saw them as evidence that *something is going on.*

That *something* appeared very good indeed. Suddenly it seemed that Einstein's question, "Is the universe friendly?" could be answered, *yes.*

THE COMING OF DISTRESS

When rumors came of disturbing experiences, no one, understandably enough, wanted very much to go looking for them. For one thing, the reports smacked of an unwelcome return to a doctrinal hell. For another, investigators are also human and were torn by the same dread that has haunted humanity throughout time; they stopped short of examining the darker side of NDEs. And for the major researchers, all of whom worked in heavily scientific academic settings, someone commented about them to me recently, "These guys were already being ostracized for the NDEs that looked like heaven; they couldn't have touched anything that might be called hell."

Furthermore, experiencers were hardly storming the telephones to report dark NDEs. How many might there be? No one knew. Only rarely would such an experience be shared, as religious studies scholar Carol Zaleski discovered in researching her groundbreaking comparison of medieval and modern NDEs: "Gone are the bad deaths, harsh judgment scenes, purgatorial torments, and infernal terrors of medieval visions; by comparison, the modern otherworld is a congenial place, a democracy, a school for continuing education, and a garden of unearthly delights" (1987, 7). Lurid accounts of hell are frequent in medieval literature, but not today. Has hell been abandoned, or do we simply refuse to talk about it?

Why such reluctance? Speaking, if I may say, from experience, one reason for the reluctance to disclose a frightening NDE is that the experience is as powerful as a pleasurable NDE, both emotionally and spiritually: to retell it is to relive it, and the idea of reliving a deeply distressing experience at the level of that literal interpretation is often unbearable. Unfortunately, no alternative explanation is easily available to average readers and watchers of television. As interpretation it might be medieval, but the terminology of heaven and hell is the only vocabulary most people know..

Another reason for the reluctance of experiencers and researchers alike is that the label the darker NDEs wore was "negative." No wonder no one wanted to go after them! Consider the equations: *blissful experience = positive / good / reward / heaven;* but *disturbing experience = negative / bad / punishment / hell.* With these equations comes judgment: a positive experience, it is assumed, indicates a positive person, someone with a highly evolved consciousness (yay!), while a negative experience points to a negative person with a lower quality of being and consciousness (boo!). Whether the event is interpreted as specifically hellish or simply as negative, only the words have changed; the judgmentalism remains as strong as ever. Would *you,* as a person with a distressing NDE, rush to tell your family, your bridge club, your pastor or attorney, or the press?

However, I can say to these temptations of easy judgment, "Wrong." This does not mean I have answers, only that there are more helpful perspectives.

PERSPECTIVES

For starters, it is untrue that only "bad" people have "bad" experiences. Saints and truly spiritual individuals of all traditions across the centuries have reported experiences of terror and despair. Further, a terrifying experience has every bit as much potential for being transformative as an encounter with the Light, although the process and the paths will be different.

Third, both the radiant and the dark experience contain seeds of temptation as well as transformation. The temptation with a pleasurable NDE is to grandiosity, ego-inflation, self-admiration for being worthy of such an exalting experience. The temptation with a terrifying experience is to spiritual paralysis and despair. The danger of yielding to any of these temptations is that it short-circuits both the message and the journey.

Taking an NDE or any of its relatives as factually and physically true suggests that it points to an external place of forces which are outside of us—the Heaven or Hell of tradition. But this is not the only possibility. Such experiences can also be interpreted as a movement inward, to a depth of self and human existence only dimly comprehensible. Either interpretation can be seen as touching something sacred. Even when an interpretation is thoroughly secular, an assumption of a purely biological event, the bottom line conclusion is almost always the same: *'Something is going on...and it's big!'*

I tend to believe that we humans are not built for having all the answers about things of that sort. Quite possibly this is merely a convenient conviction on my part, but it saves a lot of anguish about not knowing: if it's unattainable, how could we *possibly* have actual *proof* of heaven and hell as actual places? However, still wanting something to use as a handle, I have found it productive to proceed *as if* the journey were inward and to watch for the discoveries which emerge from that search. In other words, what if our search for answers takes us inside our own selves, or at least inside our own psyches? We are, after all, part of the universe and part of Creation. There are *always* discoveries.

Reality does not change because we shift terminology. It does not change because we do not like what we discover. Just as the astrophysical cosmos contains both novas and black holes, so near-death experiences show us that heaven and hell exist, whether understood as external physical realms in a religious cosmology, or as the poles of spiritual experience, or as aberrant states of consciousness. The *experiences* are real. What changes, perhaps, is our willingness to hear the words and deal with the reality. We are all of us—physicists, theologians, psychologists, NDErs, students, accountants, housewives—trying to describe the same universe.

The literature of mysticism, from all traditions the world around, is full of the recognition of *both* darkness and light as aspects of the journey. So is the literature of physics, and of the arts, and of psychology. Francesco B. DiLeo, M.D., a psychiatrist of Johns Hopkins, wrote some years back (1985):

> ... As above, so below! As external, so internal! Paradise, Hell, Purgation, Mystical Union, God, Evil, Ego-Death, Rebirth, Myths of Renewal, can no longer be dismissed as... fantasies. The mind, at its very depth, appears to connect with the vastness of outer space. Both the inner and the outer universe appear, at first, to be divided into a positive and a negative half. Both halves need to be experienced before the state of duality can be transcended.

The irony of our modern reliance on hard data and "proof" is that it has led us to forget too much and try to control too much. Agreeing to accept only the light, we have forgotten how to name our fears, have denied their existence and repressed their intensity. We have forgotten, even in most religious expression, that beyond the laboratory there are subtler routes to answers, that what is unwanted and buried becomes what may lead us home. The invitation of the terrifying NDE is to a retouching of that ancient nerve of imaginal perception, a reconnection with the entirety of human experience. Wholeness? It's time.

CHAPTER 3

What is a Distressing Spiritual Experience?

Nowhere is it written that life is serious,
though it is often hard, and even terrible.

—A NURSE AT A WORKSHOP

Not all spiritual experiences are uplifting and joyful, full of the pink clouds of so much popular writing. Some are downright terrible. But saying this leads to many questions:

How distressing is "distressing"? Just what is a "distressing near-death experience?" Spiritual is good, right, so how can there be "a bad spiritual experience"? If a person has one, that means there is something wrong about the person, right? Or maybe something evil? Is the person psychotic?

This entire book is the result of these questions. Here is how my answer begins.

Fact: The world works in ways beyond what the physical sciences describe or our everyday senses imagine.

It really is true that some psychological events are experienced as taking place in ways that are not possible in ordinary physical

21

existence. Just as in *The Wizard of Oz*, there is a sense of journeying to a strange and often exotic landscape. There may be messengers, and messages. But always, always, *it feels absolutely genuine.* This is "We're not in Kansas anymore." Some of these experiences feel so real—so "realer than real"—that it is impossible to doubt them. They look and feel like a visible, tangible reality, though they seem to exist somehow beyond the ordinary physical world. They are often described as visits to actual *places*, often thought of in Western cultures as heaven or hell. Or even not-Kansas.

A fairly reliable trigger for this kind of happening is being at least momentarily close to death, which led to the term *near-death experience.* However, virtually identical events may happen with other triggers, such as during a time of intense psychological or emotional stress; or intense physical exertion, such as in running; or during deep prayer or meditation; or during intense sex. They sometimes occur spontaneously. Such look-alike events (some call them not-near-death experiences, or nNDEs) may also be called a spiritually transformative experience (STE), extraordinary human experience (EHE), or a *conversion experience.* Sometimes an *out-of-body experience* (OBE) will have a transcendent quality and may have powerful effects. Technically speaking, all these numinous events are *mystical experiences.*

> **Note:** Because the term 'NDE' has become so familiar, I use it to apply to all these types of experience rather than exclusively to events after a cardiac arrest. This is, strictly speaking, inaccurate, and the STE acronym could be used just as well. My using a single acronym avoids throwing around a lot of multi-syllabic terms for parallel experiences. Please bear with me for the sake of word count! If your primary interest is in death *per se* rather than in this type of experience, you may find my generalizing of "NDE" irritating. I apologize.

By whatever name, the impact of such a phenomenon is deeply shocking and shatters one's sense of normalcy. As the Burmese monk discovered, it fits the shock described by psychotherapist Alex Lukeman as "the destruction of traditional and habitual patterns of perception and understanding, including religious belief structures and socially accepted concepts of the nature of human existence and behavior." (Read that again, slowly. Imagine having an experience so powerful it collapses everything you believe about the way the world works, the nature of your existence, everything that supports you in your religious and philosophical beliefs. What will you hang onto now?)

Coda: The world works in ways beyond what the physical sciences describe or our everyday senses imagine. On the other hand, although all that loss of belief must be dealt with, there are new beliefs to balance it. For instance, a common response is, "There's more! This physical world isn't all there is!" Life and the world will never be the same.

For experiencers with a wonderful NDE, the "more" is great news. In fact, the great majority of these revelations are experienced as pleasant, even blissful, although adjusting to the new understandings can be extremely difficult. However, for perhaps one in five individuals who have such an experience, it is marked by intense fear and anxiety amounting to terror. That "more" will take time, patience, and much rethinking; virtually no one will want to hear about it.

DISTRESS OR HELL?

When psychiatrist Bruce Greyson and I analyzed our findings in the first study of distressing NDEs (Greyson and Bush, 1992), we discovered that they cover a broad territory and typically fall into one of three major categories:

THE INVERTED EXPERIENCE

For many individuals, what is frightening is not *what* happens but *that* anything happens which is so far out of the norm. The pattern is the same as for pleasurable NDEs, but the person is terrified: therefore, an "inverted" response.

"What's going on? *No!* I'm *not supposed* to be up on the ceiling with my body down there on the bed. *No!* I am *not supposed* to be shooting into space! Absolutely *no!* This situation is out of control and dangerous, and I'm seeing people I know who are dead, and I've never been so scared in my life. Somebody *put me back!*"

THE VOID

Another type of distressing NDE carries a sense of total aloneness in empty, endless, featureless space, perhaps feeling abandoned in the cosmos, in what is called the Void. This is sometimes called an experience of No-Thingness, because every *thing* disappears, leaving only whatever is potential—and potential is invisible.

Imagine that you step outside your home one night, into the dark, and find everything vanished—*everything*, including the building you just left, the ground under your feet, stars, moon, people, trees, insects, your feet... It's only you—that is, your consciousness—and space. You may receive a message that earthly existence was a trick or a joke. For all you can tell, it's just *gone!*

A HELLISH NDE

The least common of the experiences is the perception of being close to—or in—hell. The sensation may begin with a sense of falling, of smelling something unpleasant, of hearing harsh noises or voices, of seeing redness and believing it to be fire—or even visualizing fire itself. Alternatively, a perception of hell may come from coldness, a barren or ugly landscape, seeing wandering, featureless people, or observing people who seem physically tormented without experiencing torment oneself. Like the monk, people often say they have a guide with them. For most experiencers, what is hellish is the fear of what might be about to happen, rather than what actually *does*, for the experience is often compared to being a tourist. On the other hand, in the intense shamanic initiation type of experience, there may be a sense of being torn apart, then reassembled and returned to a new life (the classic mystical pattern of suffering/death/resurrection).

LIFE REVIEW GUILT

A suggested fourth category involves NDEs with a life review in which the experiencer feels he or she is being negatively judged. Some people have reported feeling crippling guilt because, in a life review, they could feel every painful thing they had made others feel during their lifetime. (Think Scrooge in *A Christmas Carol.*)

An identification of hell may also come after the NDE itself, when a bewildered and frightened experiencer tries to figure out what happened, and decides it must have been hell.

NEGATIVITY?

Distressing experiences range from vaguely disturbing to deeply traumatizing, often producing characteristics of post-traumatic stress disorder (PTSD). For this reason, while pleasant NDEs are commonly referred to as "positive" events, the unpleasant ones are often called "negative," unfortunately suggesting that they are harmful and of no value.

In fact, though, like mystics through the ages, Wikipedia describes spiritual experiences as "real encounters with God or gods, or real contact with higher-order realities"; they are therefore meaningful. As a glorious light-filled NDE may represent the heights of spiritual experience, the distressing ones represent the depths. Heights or depths, they are all spiritual events.

Although the distressing events are by definition deeply painful, a person who is able (maybe brave enough) to explore carefully can discover valuable insights. What makes it hard to reach such insights is that there are different levels of meaning, and our temptation is to stop at too low a level. Richard Rohr, the Franciscan friar, author, and educator discusses this as "several levels of knowing and interpreting reality—a 'hierarchy of truths' as Pope Francis calls it." Rohr quotes the Pope:

> Not all truths are created equal, or of equal importance. Something might be true, for example, merely on a psychological level or a historical level or a mythological level, but not on a universal level. For some sad and illogical reason, fundamentalists think the historical level is the 'truest' one. 'Did it really happen just that way?' The literal level is one of the least fruitful levels of meaning. Even if it did happen just that way, our capacity to understand even that truth is still filtered through our own cultural and personal biases, which are largely unconscious. Truth on that level may be fascinating, but it seldom changes your life. (Rohr, 2013).

These events seem so *real*, as if the images and perceptions had come from a trip to a physical landscape! It is no wonder that the first interpretation is almost always literal, that least advanced level of meaning. And this often leads to the next problem for many experiencers, which is a confusion between the NDE and religious beliefs.

A BELIEF ISSUE

In describing their NDEs, people do not typically say they were taught detailed rules for what to believe or how to worship, and the beings they encounter do not wear name tags or introduce themselves. These types of experience—NDE, STE, EHE, mystical experiences, whatever—rarely teach specifics of the thinking kind that religions deal with—that is, beliefs and doctrines, rituals and activities of life in a particular system. Rather, these events operate at the deepest level of the subconscious, where everything happens in image and symbol and archetype, and which must then be interpreted. The experience, then, like life itself, consists of a series of images and possible verbal messages; but the person's interpretation will be *based on what the person knows from his or her culture and previous life learnings.*

For a person whose life experience includes being taught about a terrifying place called Hell, and who then has an NDE with feelings of fear and anxiety, it would make sense to believe they were taking place in Hell. It is at this point that doctrinal associations with hell come into play because they are so deeply embedded in Western culture. That has been ingrained into us by centuries and centuries of Western conviction (see Chapter 7). *As a culture, we rarely mention that there might be any alternative explanation; it's either hell, or you're an atheist!*

I have two problems with this: first, that people are so often crippled by fear and guilt about a supposed literal meaning of the NDE (punishment, unworthiness, blame, the wrath of God) that their life becomes deformed.

Second, an assumption that the experience as a phenomenon is really about only the afterlife precludes our learning anything of value for life, here, now, in this place. Meaningfulness gets pushed ahead until after we die. What a waste of experience!

CHAPTER 4

About the Why

The function of a distressing near-death experience is to deliver (Choose one):

A. A foretaste of punishment after death
B. An external judgment made by a spiritual superpower on the quality of one's life
C. A subconscious judgment made by oneself on the quality of one's life
D. Neither a prediction nor judgment but a symbolically coded message about something of importance to one's life
E. Other. Your suggestion

Note: In the interest of not wasting anyone's time, "A meaningless hallucination" is not included in that list.

Why does anyone have a distressing NDE rather than a lovely one? What is the function of a distressing NDE? Any honest response, of course, is rather like the answer to "Is there a God?" because however strong our convictions in any direction, none of us, now or ever, has had a *provable* reply. Data from near-death studies of the past forty years point to no indicators of who will have what kind of NDE.

What is the function of a near-death experience, then? What does it mean? What is the function of any spiritual/mystical experience? Or any dreadful, life-harming event? I don't know. However, that is not quite the same as saying, "I haven't a clue," and as four thousand years or so of theological debate have neither definitively answered the question about God nor exhausted the conversation, I figure we can at least take a crack at the question.

Our comprehension will be influenced, it seems to me, by three factors: first, antiquity—the fact that such experiences have occurred since earliest human consciousness; second, conventional wisdom, or "what everybody knows"; third, the power of emotion.

FACTOR #1: ANTIQUITY

I am convinced that it was experiences like NDEs which supported, many prehistorical ages ago, the development of doctrines of heaven and hell. Then and now, because the event is *experienced* as so phenomenally real, it has been interpreted as literally, materially real.

Add to this the empirical reality of volcanoes, demonstrating to the ancients and to any of us who watch geological events in Iceland that there really is fire underground. The perceived reality of the experiential events was processed through the universal human patterning ability and became a narrative, a story. In turn, that story form, coupled with the empirical reality of molten fires, became understood as a matter of geography rather than experience, which bequeathed to our forefathers the Hell of legend, which is how it wound up in theological arguments. If that is the way you choose to interpret this whole question, you may be dismayed to recognize that I am about to take a road less traveled.

Am I saying that hell is a lie? No. Maybe there really is such a place. But I am saying that there are other possibilities *which can only be considered if they are discussed.*

Whether one believes or dismisses a traditional view of hell, humanity is now by and large pinned against the wall of its own consciousness by the ancient and nearly universal concept that justice demands some kind of punishment for wrongdoing. Thousands of years ago that led to the conclusion that at death, the sum of our lives will be totaled up, and we will be punished for our wrongs. The very existence of debates about hell acknowledges the concept as a living idea. Believed or not, hell sits like a scowling potential somewhere in our mental set.

FACTOR #2: CONVENTIONAL WISDOM

A second mostly subliminal influence on our thinking is the conventional wisdom. This is a variant on the issue of justice. Thoroughly entrenched in human consciousness by the time the story of Job was being told some 2600 years ago, the conventional wisdom claims that good people get good stuff and bad people get bad stuff. If you have fortune, health, people who love you, a good job, and an iPad, you must be living right; you are a deserving person. On the other hand, if you're impoverished (worse than simply broke), sickly, homeless, unemployed, and non-digitized, it must be because you are undeserving: a taker, a bum, a lazy loser. If you're suffering, you must deserve it. Right? We still have political parties and even religious groups demonstrating the strength and durability of this view.

Hah. The problem with the conventional wisdom is that it's wrong as often as it's right. Maybe oftener. There is simply no evidence that being poor is always the result of laziness, or that every illness reflects on the character of the patient, or that having a distressing NDE says anything about the worthiness or social value of the person who has it. Oh, yes, it's *about* the person, but not in the judgmental sense implied by reward-punishment thinking. More on this later.

FACTOR #3: EMOTIONAL FORCE

What keeps the concept of hell pinned so strongly in us is the same aspect of consciousness that keeps memories of first love so strong, or that holds any near-death experience stable and lifelong in memory—*the power of the emotional charge.*

Any full-blown spiritual and/or near-death experience carries an earthquake's worth of emotional charge, for its experiencer most of all, but perhaps also at lower voltage for those who hear about it. When the experience is shockingly unpleasant, the charge is compounded, just as the shock of an auto accident is greater with a mangling collision rather than a fender bender, whether you're the driver or a rubbernecker. There is no loss of the fear of death in dNDEs, so death anxiety roars into play. The natural terror of being annihilated as a personal self becomes bulked up by guilt as we wonder if the experience was brought about by some unrecognized flaw in ourselves, or by something we did. The superego growls, "I've been telling you, bad, bad, bad!"—the voice of Original Sin, which has been shaping guilt in Western minds for eighteen hundred years.

When this powerful emotional charge is joined with social factors, as in #1 and #2, the stage is set for a catastrophic interpretation, an identification of hell that spans cultures. Civilization itself can be held motionless by threats of the traditional hell (as, for example, by the mass hysteria around rumors of satanic-inspired child abuse or witchcraft). Fear of non-being (ontological fear) renders otherwise sensible humans unable to think straight.

Lousy. Terror and guilt are a toxic combination; yet this notion of punishment after death is so wired into our systems, it is almost impossible to escape. It is crippling. The remedy, I believe, is to learn that there actually are other ways of thinking—and then to think them. But how to get there?

PERSPECTIVES

What are the alternatives? The myths of the world are full of stories featuring terrible dragons and monsters, threats and challenges of all kinds which a hero must meet and vanquish in order to win whatever the prize is and return with it to take up a journey-enhanced life. Unlike the ancients, we have kept the monsters and forgotten about the talisman. What if we were to look at distressing NDEs as mythic stories, telling us of puzzles to be solved, challenges to be met? Instead of punishment, which demands passivity, puzzles and challenges demand our skill and participation; they do not foster pointless guilt. What if we look for the boon to be won rather than concentrate only on the pain of the process?

NDE researcher Jim Macartney points to recent documenta-tion showing that along with post-traumatic *stress,* there are often stories of post-traumatic *growth:*

"Some people who have difficult NDEs or undergo extreme trauma, over time exhibit not only resiliency, but significant growth, even though they may remain physically, mentally or circumstantially compromised.

In fact, people transforming their life through crisis can be readily identified. They show greater compassion and empathy for others; new and greater strength (psychological toughness/resilience); greater psychological/emotional maturity; a recognition of vulnerability and struggle, and a deeper appreciation of life; new values and life priorities (less materialistic, heightened intimacy in relationships); greater existential or spiritual clarity.

Notice that Macartney did not say whether the trigger for such change will be pleasant or unpleasant; in fact, it may be either. In conventional wisdom terms, where pleasant equates to good and unpleasant to bad, this is a paradox; it makes no sense. But what if we are being called to see beyond that kind of black-and-white, dualistic thinking? In Macartney's view the paradox demonstrates how things work in "an intimately entangled universe pointing toward consciousness as the basis of all, a picture increasingly shared by scientists and mystics."

In fact, there is abundant literature proving his point. The key element is *crisis*. The precipitating event could be any revolutionizing situation—NDE, divorce, terrible medical procedure (especially in children), combat incident, spontaneous spiritual experience, surgery, natural or political disaster—any event that presents as a crisis, a point of disjuncture. In NDE terms, *crisis* is the situation itself, whether it involves a blasting away of previous assumptions by way of a trip to what might be heaven or by way of a distressing NDE which dismantles notions about the reality of existence. The crisis, *which may be either joyful or anguished*, precipitates movement toward the integration that was described in an email to me as "the tragic, joyful, soul-saving tension that is both our salvation and our damnation."

Tied to conventional wisdom, we shake our heads in frustration. It seems our challenge is simply to learn to accept a consciousness which may be beyond our pay grade to understand, but within which we craft our journeys. This is, indeed, the "intimately entangled universe."

CHAPTER 5

Fifteen Things We Know about Distressing NDEs

T here are so many points of view about near-death experiences, it can be tough to sift out facts from opinions. Here, for the sake of convenience, is a brief listing of what we can say with some confidence, based on research findings and informed opinion.

1   Reports of experiences like NDEs have come from around the world, going back into antiquity.

2   Simply being close to death is not a near-death experience. NDEs are a kind of event consisting of one or more specific features: consciousness being separate from the body (an out-of- body experience); a perception of traveling, often with a sense of speed; special qualities of light or dark; a landscape; encountering one or more religious figures, deceased family members, or spiritual presences; a life review; a perception of having great knowledge; intense emotion; very rapid thinking (hypercognition); sometimes transcendence (a sense of being beyond the physical world); a message; loss of the fear of death. An experience may include one or two of these elements or many; a single element may be powerful enough to transform

a person's life. Distressing NDE reports rarely include a life review, positive emotional tone, or loss of the fear of death; in fact, fear of death may for a while increase.

3   Although the great majority of accounts describe pleasant, even glorious, experiences, a review of the international literature on near-death experiences from 1975 through 2006 revealed that one in five may be disturbing. In an extensive Gallup survey published in 1982, as many as 28% of the reported NDEs were perhaps unpleasant and 1% were identified as specifically hellish.

4   The primary effect of any NDE is usually an explosive awareness that the physical world is only a small part of reality. *"There's more!"*

5   NDEs do not play favorites: they have been reported by people across demographic bases including age, race, ethnicity, gender, sexual preference, level of education, occupation, socioeconomic status, religious background and beliefs, level of religious activity, expectations of afterlife. Distressing NDEs appear to have the same universality as pleasant ones.

6   At least three types of distressing NDE have been identified: 1) one in which features common in pleasant NDEs are interpreted negatively; 2) the Void; 3) one in which features are perceived as hell, or suggest an impending but unseen hell. A suggested fourth type involves guilt in response to a life review.

7   An NDE is not always static but may switch from unpleasant to pleasant or, less commonly, from pleasant to distressing.

8   Concern about the implications of a distressing NDE and a fear of social stigma keep many people from reporting one.

9   A distressing NDE may produce long-lasting trauma, or, if it is well integrated, can lead to personal growth and wisdom.

10 A distressing NDE is upsetting during the experience, not only when thought about afterward.

11 The description of any NDE is dependent upon the experiencer's pre-existing mental categories and vocabulary. For instance, reports of a tunnel come from cultures with a developed infrastructure; in undeveloped areas, reports may include mention of moving through natural elongated shapes such as the neck of a gourd, the stem of a plant. Similarly, the spiritual figures reported in NDEs are not described as wearing name tags or as introducing themselves but are identified according to whatever spiritual figures are present in the experiencer's background and cognitive storehouse. For several years I thought of the figures in my NDE simply as "circles" because I did not know their identity as the Yin/Yang symbol. Any report identifying a presence by name ("I saw the Buddha in hell"; "Jesus came to me.") may or may not be factually true; nevertheless, the perception is bound up with the NDE's meaning for the experiencer.

12 There is no evidence that people "earn" their NDEs: character, personality, religious activity, and moral status have no recognized bearing on the type of NDE a person will have, though they may influence how the NDE is interpreted. Saints have reported dreadful visionary experiences. Criminals have reported glorious, life-turning NDEs. Some seemingly ordinary individuals have experienced both. This is not to suggest that morality is irrelevant, but we do well to avoid snap judgments about who gets what and why. There is at this time no actual evidence that good people get good NDEs and bad people get bad ones.

13 A distressing NDE is often interpreted as a warning, which leads many experiencers to try to identify what about their life they should change. Movement toward a strict religious affiliation is common. Others dismiss the NDE as "it was only…" something safely explainable (reductionism). Some struggle without success to find a resolution. In the absence of any

explicit study of how people cope with a distressing NDE, there is little reliable information.

14 Positive NDEs tend to convey powerful messages common to all human experience across time: a mandate to pay attention to the sacred, to be compassionate, to keep learning, and to be of service to others. Distressing NDEs are more idiosyncratic. Although the most common interpretation may be that they represent judgment, punishment, even damnation, the process of integrating the experience often leads to similar conclusions as those of positive NDEs (the importance of love, learning, service).

By contrast to this pattern, in shamanic traditions even the most harrowing of these experiences are understood as revealing the ancient spiritual pattern of suffering, death, and resurrection. (Quite obviously, the crucifixion, death, and resurrection of Jesus is a physical representation of this same pattern.) In psychological terms, this equates to profound self-examination, the disarrangement of core beliefs, and restructuring into a more comprehensive level of being in the world. When integrated into a person's conscious understandings, the process moves toward the qualities described by positive NDEs: compassion, learning, service.

15 Just as NDEs do not originate in any single culture, neither do they conform to any single doctrinal system, whether religious or secular. This often presents severe difficulties for experiencers who have depended on a set of inflexible beliefs, whether cultural, scientific, philosophical, or religious. This is why groups with a strict reliance on a particular set of teachings will deny the validity of any experience which does not reference those ideas.

CHAPTER 6

Are These Things Real?

In a particularly interesting article titled "The Realness of NDEs," journalist and blogger Robert Perry pondered the question of "why so many who have near-death experiences consider their experiences to have been 'real.'" Unless otherwise noted, all quotes below are from his article (2011).

In Perry's analysis of the NDE literature and first-person narratives, he noticed six factors that seem to bear on this question of why NDErs are so convinced of the reality of their experiences.

First, although people describe their NDEs as "happening all at once" (non-linear), their explanatory narratives follow the sequential norms of language (linear). They are not chaotic but coherent and plausible, which makes them sound real.

Secondly, they are marked by "the intensification of all aspects of the mind: awareness, thought, feeling, memory, sensation, and perception." Perry interprets this to mean something like, "If being in this environment means that I am *more* in every way, then that environment is itself probably more than the earthly environment—more real."

Perry relates that intensification of realness to the sheer power of the experience, which clinical social worker Kimberly Clark Sharp described as being like going behind Niagara Falls and feeling the rush, the power of millions and millions of gallons of water rushing down. She said, "That's what it's like to be in the light." In Perry's study, 93% of the participants agreed that "The power of my experience, which is beyond anything I've ever experienced on earth, made me absolutely sure that my experience was real."

Fourth, the occasional physical verification of out-of-body events contributes to the conviction of NDErs that these are real (as when a nurse confirms an event which happened while the experiencer was supposedly unable to see it).

Fifth, a sense of realness increases with a sense of being in more direct contact with the supposed afterlife environment: To read a story is different than to watch a film, which is different than to see something happening in our presence. "As the directness of contact increases, so does our trust in what we perceive."

And finally, "There may be some indefinable sense of realness that does not fall under the previous five headings, some subjective sense that, at least for the present, can't be nailed down."

In other words, because a high percentage of near-death accounts include reports of these perceptions, Perry finds common and plausible reasons to believe that near-death experiences are real.

But what does that mean? What is it, to be real?

WHAT IS IT TO BE REAL?

Three sentences in Perry's article practically jumped off the page at me.

> "We clearly need to look to hard evidence, and not just trust the subjective impression of the experiencers themselves... They are overwhelmingly convinced that their experience was real. If we can gain some genuine understanding of why, then perhaps that will help us decide how much we can believe them."

Read one way, there is an implication in this statement that, if experiencers cannot return from their NDEs with hard evidence in hand, they are perhaps not to be believed. Read slightly differently, it seems to suggest that individuals *do* return from their experiences with 'hard evidence' of materialist truth, something like lab data, in their conviction. Perhaps the hard evidence about them resides in the percentages by which experiencers have a clear perception that a 'something'—call it x—is happening.

Perry is not the only one to wonder about the reality of these kinds of experience. By contrast and from a highly informed perspective, mythologist Joseph Campbell described their nature as originating in a "metaphysically grounded realm beyond space and time, which, since it is physically invisible, can be known only to the mind" (1986). In other words, Campbell's reality need not be physical.

That is one of those statements which needs mulling over but which seems to fit with what Perry is demanding. "Something physically invisible which can be known only to the mind" seems a far more compatible approach to something as elusive as NDEs or any internal event. What hard evidence can there be about a subjective experience?

If a perception is materially unverifiable, does that mean it is false? If, as you die, your last flicker of cognition is that you are being greeted by the person you most love in all the world, how much does a researcher's opinion matter? As the experience of your last thought, the greeting is real.

HOW MUCH CAN WE KNOW?

How much can we know about these odd events? Neuroscientist and neurotheologian Andrew Newberg has intensively studied the brains of monks and nuns during peak instances of meditation and prayer. The meditators described their altered states of mind as being the absorption of the self into something larger.

Newberg reports that those altered states were not "the results of emotional mistakes or simple, wishful thinking, but were associated instead with a series of observable neurological events, which, while unusual, are not outside the range of normal brain function" (2008).

In other words, those "observable neurological events"—the hard evidence of data from brain scans—demonstrate that something measurable (i.e., "real") is happening in our familiar time/space universe; they give satisfyingly concrete data about when and where the activity occurs. However, just as a map is not the territory, the scans are incomplete. They are not the *experience*, any more than a book of photos can produce the roar and vibration of a trip to Niagara Falls.

In that same way, a near-death experience is a real experiential event—but only in the life of the individual who has it. The problem with subjective events is that only one person owns the "subject"; science depends on corroboration, but for this there are no witnesses. The reality of the NDE event shifts in the very instant when an experiencer begins to describe it, for that is when the *experience* is transformed into a conceptually ordered and interpreted *narrative* that can be described but not known and felt in all its dimensionality by anyone else in the world.

Of course the narrative is coherent; that is the business of language and reason; yet to force an experience down through the restrictiveness of language and concept is like trying to draw an accurate picture of sunrise with no colored crayons. Dawn may be suggested but cannot be captured.

LIVING IN THE REALITY OF 'ONLY IN YOUR MIND'

To make matters worse, we have to deal with Campbell's *"realm beyond space and time, which, since it is physically invisible, can be known only to the mind,"* This realm lives not in the everyday world but in the imaginal function of the unconscious, not by the sharp lines of denotation but the soft blur of connotation. This is where the archetypes live, not in the sense of neatly lined up definitions but as limitless cascades of suggestion and possibility. In common usage, saying, "It's only in your mind" means that something is unreal; but here, in Campbell's realm, only the mind can know what is true. Something may be factually wrong yet experientially or symbolically true. (As best example: Genesis, chapters 1 & 2)

A sophisticated young blogger makes some useful observations:

> For the Pentecostal Christian communities in the bush in Africa, the spiritualist aboriginal cultures in the Pacific islands, and the Shamanistic nature religions in the remote mountains of South America, humans and spirits walk the same ground and live life side by side in a way a westerner cannot fully grasp. Seemingly miraculous healings/ exorcisms/ demon sightings can and do occur—any cultural anthropologist will tell you this. But you will find alongside the "spiritual" explanation a "scientific" one that accounts for the same phenomena through psychology, deceit, or nature. Acknowledging these other explanations should not force us to choose either side. It should simply make us wary when determining what can and cannot exist based solely off of what we can and cannot observe in the material realm (Carlson, 2008).

We will continue to drive ourselves crazy if we do not recognize that the reality of the "real world" of material, physical objects does not always accurately describe the "real world" of invisible, interior personal experience which happens somewhere (and somehow) in our mind.

We must learn to live with NDEs as we do with subatomic particles, which disappear when observed; their portraits show not the particles themselves but only where they have been. Similarly, there may be no known physical, geographical locality that matches what is described in an NDE. On the other hand, NDEs have demonstrable consequences that are often real enough to disrupt and reshape human lives—the "footprints" of experiential reality. Can we accept those as convincing data?

Can we believe what experiencers say about their NDEs? Are they real? Well, do you mean, in a Western sense, are they materially *verifiable,* or are they meaningfully *true*? To mistake the difference is to create a great distortion.

The materialist view of the past four-hundred-plus years has been to insist that only the physical reality is "real" reality. This has been ferociously defended during the past century. Anything left hanging over the sides of the materialist box is derisively dismissed as illusion, as with the scorn magician and professional skeptic James Randi directs toward the spoon-bending claims of Uri Geller. In fact, the problem may be with our understanding of how to listen. When our culture says, "It's all in your mind," what if that's where this particular reality *is?*

CHAPTER 7

Being PC about
a Tough NDE

A disturbing pattern has been emerging in some readers' responses to my blog *dancingpastthedark.com.* Several readers have expressed discomfort and even anger that we actually talk about distressing NDEs! The objections seem to stem from two theoretical sources.

POLITICAL CORRECTNESS

One stream of objections rises in the notion that unpleasant NDEs represent a kind of control mechanism thought up by unnamed powers (often simply "religion") to keep people in line by fear. The experiences, though internal, are therefore seen as forces of external manipulation and abuse, which ought not to be given attention. They represent oppression.

The writers' feelings range from exasperation to outright anger, their comments including words such as "falsity," "manipulation," "intimidation," "coercion," "judgmentalism," "control." One respected reader wonders why the discussion even needs to be continued, because it gives the 'forces of oppression' such consideration rather than denouncing them outright.

CONSEQUENCES

A second type of objection stems from the assumption that "like attracts like." If we think positively, we will attract only positive influences; if we think bleak, hateful, fearful, unloving thoughts, we will attract those things to us. And by corollary, if we have distressing NDEs, it is because we drew them to us. (I have never seen any recognition of the fact that this suggests something very close to possession.) I find this altogether inadequate as explanation for a highly complex phenomenon.

A clear line can be seen running to this assumption from the oldest ideas of justice, that virtue will be rewarded and misbehavior punished—in other words, "good goes with good, and bad goes with bad," or "negative goes with negative." Unarguably, this idea is ancient. There are elements in the Hammurabi code of 3000 BCE, and it can be seen in Plato in the fifth century BCE. It is central to the biblical book of Deuteronomy, with its pages of conditional rewards and punishments, and to the story of good-guy Job, whose friends insist he must have sinned greatly to have so many misfortunes in his life. And yes, we encounter this same idea today, in the popularity of the notion that the kind of spiritually transforming experience you have is controllable, determined by something qualitative about your spiritual life, or your ordinary level of consciousness, or what you believe, or what you expect to have happen at death. The premise tends to suggest contagion, as if suffering can be caught like measles, or perhaps magnetism, so that if you give any attention to difficult ('negative') forces in order to understand them, you may be pulled into them, as if by the old Scottie dog magnets.

Of course there is a certain amount of truth to the argument. Pleasant people tend to be treated pleasantly. Consistently angry people get into more fights. But when carried to extremes or believed inflexibly, the idea not only does not support justice but actively fosters *in*justice by blaming the innocent for their misfortunes. It can also become a too-handy argument for avoidance of uncomfortable truths. Because of this idea, a great many individuals have declined to approach the topic of distressing NDEs and anything that is not focused totally on the Light.

Well, here's why I disagree with all such arguments.

For one thing, they make no allowance for mischance. Accidents. Potholes. Being struck by lightning. That…stuff happens. That good people get terrible diseases. That terrible people win the lottery. That people who follow all the rules and believe all the right things do not always win. A friend sent me an email yesterday; he said, "Our lives are uncertain and unpredictable. Love…" Yes. And uncertainly and unpredictably, some folks have really difficult near-death experiences that throw them for a loop.

Like lots of foundational stuff, these next three paragraphs may seem obvious, but they bear specifying.

Negatively judgmental attitudes toward a distressing experience (and what is worse, toward the experiencer) strongly bias everyone's response to the event and the cultural interpretation made of it. It is exactly these experiences—the difficult ones—which most need to be talked about and moved toward integration! There are floods of opinions but a drought of data to suggest why people have the type of NDE they do. A person having any near-death experience is registering a cognitive event which is very real in itself, as an experience. It has related consequences which are often life-shaping. Hyperemotional revulsion or disapproval toward the very concept of such experiences is not in any way helpful to dealing with them. Negativity is at best an ironic response to a phenomenon considered "negative."

True NDEs are not intentionally manufactured! They are internal and involuntary, the product of the human imaginal system; they are not consciously "made up," either by today's commenters or by medieval theologians. As images, the content of a distressing experience may have observable connection to the person's culture and beliefs, or it may be unfamiliar and without precedent. However, afterwards, when words are chosen to describe the event, they will come from what the person already knows; it will be culture that speaks. We learn culture through language and activities, both of which point to discussion. Discussion, and debate, and sharing of ideas and knowledge, and questioning and answering. Nothing is gained by silencing issues, even when they are painful. And if we are to be able to counter vestiges of medieval thinking, discussion is vital.

Just as putting water into a freezer produces ice, putting an experience into words solidifies the memory, producing not the experience but a story about it. The NDE cannot be known to anyone else as it is remembered by the experiencer. That person must shape the story according to the remembered emotional tone and will interpret it according to whatever came through the cultural filter during the experience. Additional meanings may be added later, as the story is processed by the experiencer and those who hear it. Eventually, it will take its place either within a local system of cultural understanding or as an outlier having no recognized explanation. Without the friction of interchange, culture withers. Without the irritation of new and sometimes unwelcome information and alternative ideas, ignorance flourishes. For affected individuals, this is often crippling.

These distinctions matter.

It has never been my intent to glorify distressing NDEs (logic fails at this notion). Nor do I wallow in fear and unhealthy emotional states; the entire point is to get beyond that. In these decades of persisting with thinking and studying and talking about distressing NDEs, my intention has steadily been, for my own sake and for the sake of others, to understand them, to move one step at a time, as if on a journey, to get down underneath all the preconceptions and assumptions, all the theories and doctrines, and ask, 'What is bedrock?' Is it possible to get beyond overlays of supposition to something so simple I am able to trust it? Can we begin to see these near-death experiences through lenses other than doctrine or distaste or disbelief?

Silence is not a natural response when trying to understand a complex experience. Silence cannot produce new knowledge or comprehension. Rejecting discussion on the grounds that one disapproves of the topic is equivalent to taking a *doctrinal* position, which is exactly what I hope to avoid.

FIVE STAGES

I see at least five natural stages in the life cycle of any NDE: experiencing, reporting, interpreting, assigning meaning, and finally, in some cases, dogmatizing.

The person who had the experience may participate in all five stages, but the first two (experiencing and reporting) are unshareable and belong to him or her alone. The third and fourth stages (interpreting and assigning meaning) are likely to be influenced by other people over time, through conversation and shared information. As any particular NDE and NDEs in general become known beyond the individual experiencer's immediate circle, they leave the 'ownership' of the experiencer and become subject to public opinion. From this stage onward, the public's conclusions about the meaning of the NDE may be quite different from the meaning held by the original experiencer.

Further, that original NDE cannot be evaluated in the terms of later stages. Any attempt to explain an NDE can come only after the experience itself, after its origination as images and emotions; with the rarest of exceptions, it does not *originate* in religious dogma or cultural ideologies, or as words and stories. Claiming that a distressing NDE must be understood as primarily an example of religious manipulation or institutional control puts a very big cart in front of this horse. What I am doing here is parsing out the NDE and its very earliest stages. The recent complaints are directed toward the interpretation and institutionalization of NDEs—responses to which the writers may quite rightly object— yet we reach the dogmatisms of stage 5 only by first going through the experience (stage 1) and its interpretive steps. The process *demands* conversation, informed discussion, and differences of opinion. The notion that distressing experiences indicate manip- ulation, coercion, control, as well as attempts at censoring—the whole range of power plays—no, these are *effects* as much as are post-NDE psychic sensitivities or PTSD. They are extremely late- stage phenomena.

As I use the term 'dogmatism,' I mean the stage at which any external and inflexible ideological belief becomes attached to an aspect of an NDE or NDEs in general. It may be secular or religious. Dogmatism differs from simply 'meaning' in that it is inflexible. A dogmatic position may be taken by an individual or a group, and even by an entire population. Dogmatisms can be wrong: "If an NDE is reported by someone who was not pronounced clinically dead, it isn't a real NDE"; "Only pleasant NDEs are real NDEs." "Anyone who has a distressing NDE must have done something to deserve it"; "NDEs are meaningless hallucinations."

I consider it merely a dogmatism, and an unhealthy one, to claim that discussion of distressing NDEs is inappropriate, or that it is by nature "negative" in the sense of 'unworthy.' That view is reminiscent of the conviction of many idealistic new parents that if their toddler is kept away from fairy tales and hears only sunny, uplifting non-fiction, there will never be fears of a monster in the closet. Nope. Doesn't work. The monsters are built in, nat- ural residents of every baby psyche. In fact, it is by dealing with the seemingly nasty stories that children begin to learn, even that young, how to deal with painful human realities.

That is the core truth: that there *are* painful human realities, many of them unmerited. Fleeing from even the idea of them is not an answer; attempting to control them by ritual and approved beliefs has never been shown to be possible.

I want to get as close as possible to answers about them. That I do not expect a complete understanding is irrelevant; I need more than what is here now, which means that discussion is imperative. The ensuing conversation will almost certainly contain errors and downright stupid claims to be discarded (some of them no doubt originating with me), but will also result in an enlightened understanding.

As psychotherapist Miriam Greenspan (read her book!) says, we must get through the grief and questions first, the agony of ego and the smaller self, to find the larger Self beyond ego. "When the ego is shattered, the heart of Love is found in this brokenness, where we least expect it" (*Healing through the Dark Emotions*, 2003, 43). But if there is no discussion, no roadway to the larger vision, how can one find an alternative to harmful explanations? In other words, like them or not, these types of experience happen; if the concept of hell is too distasteful to accept, conversation can help move us to identify a better understanding.

For many, the notion that there might be an alternative way of thinking about such torment is new information, and powerful. It takes time to soak in. It is like looking for the tiger in a photo of jungle leaves and flowers. The only way to find it may be by taking the picture apart one leaf at a time. The floor here is covered in leaves.

PART II

HELL

CHAPTER 8

Untangling Hell

*Do you believe in hell? Even if you don't, you know about it.
Even if you are sure it's no more than a fairy tale or a bunch of
manipulative social jargon, you may still feel an occasional chill.
It's so old, and so widespread... Could any of it be somehow true?*

*This is probably the best known of the essays in this book,
having been posted as "Untangling Hellish Visions" on
both the blog and the Dancing Past the Dark website.
Because it is foundational, here it is again.*

We're in a difficult position these days for talking about hell because of the current tumult about the role of religion. This is a first in human cultural history, because for somewhere between 10,000 and 100,000 years, religion has been the foundation on which people—entire peoples, in fact—built their lives. For all those hundreds of human generations, religion has supplied the stories that explain the way the world works: who is in charge, and where did we come from, and where are we going, and why are we here, and what does it all mean?

Right now, in many quarters traditional Western religion and its ancient stories have become suspect. After two thousand years, Christendom is being displaced from center stage, and we don't know what's coming to take its place.

We're between stories. Great sweeps of people are saying, 'I'm not religious; I'm spiritual.' But the thing is, *our culture is still lived against a background of the stories of the religions that built the culture.* So, even if you know little if anything about any religion and nothing about the actual traditions of hell, you may have a definite conviction about whether you believe in it or not. Everyone's thinking gets shaped around the concept.

EARLY AFTERLIFE

From the beginning of human awareness, it has been clear that everyone and everything eventually dies. But because human beings are conscious, we have always wondered, "And then what?"

In the beginning, or at least the beginning of all the enduring religious traditions, there was no clear sense of what an afterlife might be like. Despite that, at least the Indian, Babylonian, Persian, Egyptian, Greek, and Hebrew traditions shared a common thought: the dead had to go *someplace*. And so, all across the Ancient Near East came the idea of an underworld, a geographic region for the dead. In Hebrew, the region of the dead was called Sheol. The Greeks called it Hades. Same place. Everyone went there after death, good and bad, rich and poor, everyone.

Tanakh, Jewish Bible, Old Testament

What happened in Sheol, if anything did, was described only vaguely. For a couple of thousand years the underworld was imagined as being a dim and gloomy place where nothing much went on. In one Bible story, King Saul consults a medium to bring up the prophet Samuel for a consultation; but otherwise, Sheol is undisturbed. Punishment was not its job. It was simply a warehouse for the dead.

Yahweh (Jehovah, God) was concerned with how people lived their life, not what happened after death. God rewarded and punished during a person's lifetime, not after death, and he rewarded and punished the nation more than individuals; so the ultimate punishment was understood as death or national destruction, not eternal torment. The idea of torment in Sheol is never mentioned in the books of the Bible attributed to Moses or in the early Prophets. In thirty-one places in the Tanakh, the Jewish Bible, the Hebrew word is *Sheol;* yet Christian Bibles say *hell.*

THE BEGINNINGS OF HELL

Hell, it seems, is a developmental notion. The idea of punishment after death came with civilization.

Conflict

As civilizations grew, so did conflict. First with individuals, then clans, then nations, there was competition. Power struggles. By the time city-states became empires, the tensions of oppression, conscription, slavery increased people's suffering and anger.

Justice

Some four thousand years ago, in the Fertile Crescent of Mesopotamia, where Iraq and Iran are today and westward to Syria and Palestine and Egypt, nations began developing law codes. The Babylonian code was the first, followed over 500 or so years by the Hittite code of laws, the Assyrian laws, and the one best known to us, the Law of Moses. As expectations for conduct and business dealings were written, ideas about civic responsibility were accompanied by ideas about redress: if wrongs could not easily be made right, at least the persons responsible for wrongs would be punished. It was the development of a way of thinking about justice that would be projected onto God.

Dualism

In one of those countries, Persia (today Iran), the idea of dualism was articulated—the idea that everything has an opposite, from left/right and up/down to yes/no, and on to the belief that the cosmos is in eternal struggle between opposing sides: a force of divine light and goodness opposed to a force of darkness and misery, good and evil, above and below, this life and afterlife, paradise and hell. Matched pairs of good and evil on all sides. Think Luke Skywalker and Darth Vader, Harry Potter and Lord Voldemort. Fire, which purifies, indicated the presence of the good. The fire that purified objects on earth could purify souls in the afterlife. Eventually, that fire would be lighted in Sheol.

Apocalypse

Along with dualism, the Persian religion, Zoroastrianism, introduced the concept of apocalypse. The word means literally, "making wonderful," or what we might call "the fix." Apocalyptic thinking comes into play when things are so bad it seems that only divine intervention can set things right.

In the Zoroastrian view, disorder in the world outweighs order and evil outweighs good; but eventually, justice will be done. After death, people will be judged on the character of their lives and will be rewarded or purified according to the degree of their goodness or wickedness. In the final days, a savior will come to defeat evil and lead the world into a new age. All suffering, illness, and death will end forever; the dead will come back to life; and everyone who is faithful to the teachings will enter into a Golden Age of bliss. Those who do not agree will be purified in a river of molten metal.

Leaving out that river of molten metal, this should sound oddly familiar. Explanation: About 2,500 years ago, in one of a long series of invasions and conquests that tormented the eastern coast of the Mediterranean, the Persian Empire took over what had been Hebrew territory and ruled for almost two hundred years. Most Persian kings treated their conquered peoples decently (at least compared to others), and numbers of the Judaic educated population achieved responsible positions in government and civic affairs, where there was exchange of ideas.

The concepts of dualism and apocalypse stuck and became part of later Jewish thought, as we can see in the continuing influence of those and other Persian ideas across the centuries. Here, from a fundamentalist Christian writer today is an example of that dualistic thinking:

> If Hell or the Lake of fire doesn't exist, then there cannot be a Gospel at all. The fact that there is a Gospel demands the existence of a place called Hell and the Lake of fire. The term "Gospel" is understood as "good news"—the good news of salvation…However if there is "good news" to proclaim then it is logically reasonable to proclaim the "bad news" or else our so-called good news would be totally irrelevant… But if there is a Gospel…then this demands the existence of a place called Hell (*Angelfire*).

The Book of Enoch

Couple Zoroastrian ideas like the conflict between good and evil, existence of a distinct heaven and hell, and judgment in the End Time together with a violent and turbulent present, and what will result? For the Jewish people remembering exile and living with oppression, one result was a fiery passion for justice expressed in over-the-top apocalyptic language.

All these influences come together in the curious Book of Enoch, the oldest known Jewish work not included in the Bible.

Although non-canonical, Enoch was a hugely popular and influential tale of how a group of angels rebelled against God and led the people of Earth into wicked behaviors (including harlotry and eye shadow). Sheol, it says, is now divided into three areas: one for the righteous; a second for sinners who were punished for their wrongdoings while on earth; and the third for the wicked who received no earthly punishment and will share the same fate as the disobedient angels. God appoints the archangel Michael ("field commander for the army of God"[1]) to bind the fallen angels: "In those days they shall be led off to the abyss of fire: (and) to the torment and the prison in which they shall be confined forever. And whosoever shall be condemned and destroyed will from thenceforth be bound together with them to the end of all generations."

Scholars agree that the literature of this period shows the tensions created by the conflicts of the time. God's justice and nurturance sat on one side, with the desperate conditions of daily reality on the other. Envisioning the all-too-real cruelties of physical life into an afterlife for the wicked provided a sense of vengeance. It was the dark side of justice becoming visible.

The Greeks and Romans: Hades

After two centuries of relatively quiet Persian rule, the Greek military genius Alexander swept his troops across the Mediterranean. Over the next two hundred years we see a swirl of cultures and philosophies: the earthy pragmatism of Jewish thought; the dualism and apocalyptic imagery of Zoroastrianism; then an aggressive Greek passion for human reason, art, philosophy, and their gods and goddesses. Some of the Greek religions agreed strongly with Zoroaster that justice meant punishing evildoers. Their myths included the tale of a pit at a level deep below Hades, called Tartarus, where a group of rebellious semi-divinities was incarcerated—a Greek version of the Enoch story. Conflict over Hellenistic philosophies would create deep divisions in the Jewish community, some of whom would adopt Greek ideas about punishment in the afterlife.

Romans and the Battle of Jerusalem

Another two hundred years, and in 63 BCE the Greeks were overthrown by the Romans. Rome brought military power and emphasis on law and order. But order in that region was always an overlay, with unrest just beneath the surface.

By the turn into what we call the Common Era, two thousand years of invasions and war and murderous internal feuds had brutalized the Mediterranean world. Roman rule was harshly authoritarian. An extravagantly wealthy Jewish ruling class cooperated with the Romans, disdaining the much larger number of Jews who were abjectly, desperately poor. Oppression was the name of the game. Punishment for even minor wrongdoing was harsh, often hideous. Guerilla bands of zealots wanting revolution hid in the hills, making forays against the tyrannical military occupation. With tensions so high, apocalyptic thought was everywhere, swept by rumors of a messiah coming to overthrow the Roman oppressors.

JESUS

In that environment in the year 33 CE (Common Era), the Jewish healer, teacher, and prophet Jesus of Nazareth was convicted of treason for complex political and religious reasons.

Jesus was a visionary of extraordinary personal charisma and such immense spiritual power that the tradition of his divinity would grow as years went on. He healed by touch and at a distance, and by casting out demons, the first century's understanding of mental illness. He said he was bringing the Kingdom of God on earth. In his dynamic teaching he was unafraid to dispute with religious authorities, saying that Israel must consider the spirit as well as the letter of their Moses-given laws, and that the nation would be destroyed if it continued to ignore loving God and caring for each other, especially the poor and marginalized, which was at the heart of the teachings.

By championing the poor and the marginalized rather than the power-brokers, Jesus went up against the power structure of both the Jewish hierarchy and the Roman oppressors. He was crucified as a common criminal by the Roman authorities and died; but on several occasions later he was reportedly seen, living, by his students and followers, who believed him to be the Messiah, the long-hoped-for savior of Israel. Within a few years, his followers would believe him to be divine.

THE WRITINGS

Paul

The first surviving writings about Jesus came some twenty to thirty years after his death, letters from the traveling missionary Paul to early groups of Jesus-followers around the eastern Mediterranean. Paul, who did not know Jesus in life, had a life-changing NDE-like vision of the glorious risen Christ. He expected the Christ to return at any moment, bringing in the Kingdom of God. God, Paul wrote, will render spiritual judgment; the wicked will be quickly destroyed, and non-believers will simply die and disappear. Eternal physical torment is not part of Paul's message.

In Paul's letters we see how Greek influence has been overtaking Hebrew thought: here, for the first time, what to *believe* is as important as how to *live*. That will become central in the next several centuries.

The Gospels

After Paul, the next writings are the four accounts known as the Gospels. They were not written until forty years and more after Jesus's death, quite possibly to save his teachings as the first generation of followers was dying off. They were most probably written between the destruction of Jerusalem in the year 70 CE and the end of the first century. The first three documents, titled Mark, Matthew, and Luke, are not biographies of Jesus but records of his activities and some of his sayings; they were written for specific groups of followers and reflect their perspectives. By contrast, the book of John is a spiritual reflection.

What do they say about hell? Except for Matthew, the life of the world to come is mentioned only in passing, and then primarily regarding what rank the disciples might have in the Kingdom—who would sit where. Jesus spent far less time talking about the final destiny of the wicked than one would think, considering the amount of discussion since then. What he warned about was that Israel would be destroyed if its people did not change their hearts and ways. (They didn't, and it was.)

Mark

The Gospel of Mark, the earliest of the three, was written around the time the Temple was destroyed, roughly forty years after Jesus' death. In a series of warnings to Israel, Jesus mentions Gehenna once, quoting Isaiah (Is 66:44). (See the section on Gehenna, below.) The basic message of Mark establishes Jesus's prophetic teaching that for those who pay no attention to the needs of others, there will be consequences.

Matthew

The Gospel of Matthew, c. 80-85 CE, is based almost entirely on Mark. Like the other gospel writers, Matthew expects Jesus to return any day now, bringing the end time and inaugurating the Kingdom of Heaven, which is what other writers mean by the Kingdom of God. (Writing primarily to Jewish audiences, Matthew minimizes the use of the divine name). He knows about the devastation of the Temple and Jerusalem, the madness of Nero, and seems to be writing during the early bloody persecutions of Christ-followers (many of whom were Jews). Not surprisingly, he includes earnest moral teachings and warnings of peril on all sides, with a definite awareness of suffering and all too real tortures.

Matthew mentions Satan, but only as the adversary who tests Jesus in the wilderness. In Matthew 25:30, Jesus refers to "the outer darkness" where "men will weep and gnash their teeth," which can be interpreted as an earthly outcome within the story he is telling, as well as afterlife. Eleven verses later, he speaks of the "the eternal fire prepared for the devil and his angels" but says nothing about including humans.

In the Gospels, Jesus makes eleven referrals to Gehenna; seven of the mentions are in Matthew, all of them predicting desperate suffering, not necessarily after death. Alice Turner (1993, 54) says, "Matthew's great innovation was to attach eschatological (end time) warnings to the parables Mark attributed to Jesus. It is Matthew who establishes in the Christian mind that not to be saved is desperately perilous." Salvation begins to tip from being about the well-being of the entire nation to being about individuals.

Luke

The Gospel of Luke, with its sister volume the Acts of the Apostles, was written toward the end of the first century CE. In this Gospel, Jesus tells a Jewish version of a popular story in which Hades has separate sections of comfort and torment. A homeless and ill beggar, Lazarus (not Jesus's friend Lazarus, whom he reportedly raised from the dead), has been lying outside a rich man's house. He dies, and angels carry him to Hades, where he is comforted by Abraham himself. The rich man, who is not even named in the story, also dies and goes to Hades, but gets no angels and awakens in fiery torment. He sees Abraham a distance away, with the beggar. He begs Abraham to "send Lazarus, that he may dip the tip of his finger in water, and cool my tongue; for I am tormented in this flame." Abraham says, 'Child, remember that during your life you received your good things, and likewise Lazarus bad things; but now he is being comforted here, and you are in agony.'"

The story line of a poor versus a rich man was popular in Jewish folktales of the period. Jesus reworks it, adding details that turn it into a subtle critique about the Jewish ruling class as well as a moral tale about greed. (Notice that the issue is not punishment but greed and fairness, balance: you had your turn, now Lazarus has his turn.)

Although widely read as meaning that Jesus was teaching about hell, that misses the point that Jesus was actually telling a parable about the link between God's requirements and treatment of others, with a dig at religious leaders who were ignoring both. There is a very wide range of interpretations of the story. A fascinating article about it is online at *http://www.truthaccordingto-scripture.com/documents/death/the-rich-man-and-lazarus-dawson.php*

John

Gospel of John: circa 100 CE. John never mentions hell but uses "heaven" nineteen times, not as a place to which people are headed but as the source of spiritual good.

Gehenna

Across the books of Matthew, Mark, and Luke, Jesus uses the word *Gehenna* eleven times. His listeners knew it well as a valley just outside Jerusalem, the "Valley of Slaughter," a place of horror. It had been the site of a temple to the Canaanite god, where drums drowned out the shrieks of babies being roasted alive on the out-stretched hands of a bronze furnace as sacrifice to Moloch. After the temple was torn down, the valley was considered cursed, an abomination, and Gehenna became associated with violent suffering and destruction. The prophet Jeremiah (Jer 7:30-33) warned the people of Jerusalem that because they were not honoring their covenant, not living according to Torah, they would be destroyed like Gehenna. In English Bibles, the word appears as "hell."

Quite a good discussion of Gehenna is available at the Wikipedia site: *https://en.wikipedia.org/wiki/Gehenna*

One persisting tradition says that Gehenna became the city's garbage dump, where fires burned continually and the worst refuse was thrown, including the bodies of animals and criminals. While some scholars have pointed out that no archeological findings justify that idea, there is evidence of its use for human sacrifice. With or without the burning dump, Gehenna was infamous as a hideous and abominable place of defilement, violence, and death.

A close reading of the contexts in which Jesus mentioned Gehenna shows that we should not be too quick to assume he meant it as hell in our sense, either in its details or in its purpose as afterlife. For one thing, Jesus did not teach personal afterlife the way later theologians would, and the concept of eternal physical torment would not exist for another three hundred years. When Jesus used Gehenna as a threat, the context addressed the *nation of Israel* to say that if the leaders, the priests, and the people did not take responsibility for keeping the teachings to bring about the Kingdom of God *in this world* (love God, love the neighbor, and care for the needy), Israel would be destroyed *as if it were thrown into Gehenna.*

Israel did not listen. In the year 70 CE the nation experienced the violent and fiery destruction of Jerusalem and most of the Temple, a bloody massacre of the city's Jewish population, and a dispersal of survivors as slaves. That catastrophic downfall was Jesus's vision— Israel's Gehenna. The judgment and punishment of *individuals* as interpreted by later theologians were never a part of Jesus' teaching.

The worm that does not die

What about the verses in Mark (9:43-48) that sound as though corpses will be forever chewed by worms in an eternal fire? Jesus warns his listeners to be wary of "Gehenna, where their worm does not die and the fire is not quenched." Isn't this a description of our idea of hell?

Actually, Jesus is quoting from the book of Isaiah, verses 66:23-24 (whose idea of an afterlife would have been Sheol, not hell), describing the scene after an uprising: "And they [living people] will go out and look on the dead bodies of those who rebelled against me; the worms that eat them will not die, the fire that burns them will not be quenched, and they will be loathsome to all mankind."

Explanation: There are so many unburied corpses on the battlefield that maggots will have plenty of food and will not die (but will become pupa and then flies, creating more maggots). Not until the corpses have been entirely devoured will the fires burn out on their own, without being quenched.

Loathsome goes without argument, but there is no need to read eternity into the words. The bodies in Isaiah are clearly physical, lying on a battlefield and being chewed and burned in this world, not in an afterlife.

No matter how much the people of later centuries would do so, it is always a mistake to read biblical words out of context. In these verses Mark quotes Jesus not as talking about our idea of hell, and not about individual belief or behavior. The verses come from a section in which Jesus is talking about risks to the entire community; he is making an emotional point rather than a logically descriptive one, and his reference to Isaiah is part of its emotional power. It is likely that Mark's audience would have recognized the urgency of his message, because for previous religious leaders (the echo is of traditional Jewish priests), maiming would be a dreadful fate, destroying their priestly function. Jewish faith is always concerned with the conditions of life in this world, as theologian Andrew Perriman notes:

> The vivid prophetic language in which these events are described already foreshadows the visions of impending judgment that we find in the New Testament. The point to stress is that in the scriptures Jesus was quoting, this

language always has reference to historical events seen from the perspective of Israel's unique existence. It has to be unequivocally demonstrated, therefore, and not merely assumed, that the authors of the New Testament used this language in a fundamentally different sense to speak of post-historical or metaphysical realities. In my view this cannot been demonstrated. The New Testament is as much focused on the historical existence of the people of God as is the Old Testament.

The Gospel conclusion

Throughout the four gospels, it is clear that there are serious repercussions for unfaithful behavior of the nation and its members; however, afterlife judgment and punishment as interpreted by later theologians do not appear. This does not lessen God's determination that his people will live righteously. There will be consequences, including physical destruction; but God does not torment forever and ever.

The conclusion is unmistakable: the hell of later centuries was never the point of Jesus' teaching or message. What he wanted was for people to change their lives now, here, to love God with all their heart, soul, strength, and mind, and to take as good care of their neighbors as they did themselves. If they did not, there would be a price; but nowhere in Jesus' teachings is there anything like afterlife hell as it has come to be known. Unfortunately, with the passage of time, cultural forces grew louder than the voice of the messenger.

Revelation

The closing book of the New Testament is Revelation, the vision of an unknown author, traditionally thought to be John of Patmos. Written 70 – 80 years after Jesus's death, Revelation is the primary source for most of our popular notions of hell, including the lake of fire. Revelation began as a vision and became apocalyptic literature, messages full of elaborate symbols and images. We are so accustomed to scientific fact, we do not deal well with symbols these days, which is why Revelation's lurid apocalyptic style has led one gifted writer to describe it as "John has a nightmare in a cave, in which gentle Jesus is impersonated by a divine sadist" (R.F. Dietrich).

Suppose that 2,000 years from now an audience were to watch one of today's superhero movies and conclude that we believe it as factual. That is what we do to Revelation. Remember, when Revelation was written at the end of first century or early in the second, it was a terrible time—violent, bloody, cataclysmic. Most people were impoverished, many were refugees. Judaism had been turned upside down, and now Jewish and gentile interpretations of Jesus were fought over, often violently. There were persecutions of Christians, some of whom were eaten by dogs or lions, or set aflame as torches. No wonder the vision that became Revelation combines a fantasy of vindictiveness with a dream of rescue.

"They shall be tormented by fire..."

The only five references to a lake of fire appear in Revelation. Elaborate images and symbols pump up the emotional level of the work. The visuals are memorable, some beautiful and others horrible, often violent and sometimes vicious. Like other apocalyptic literature, the language is cryptic, metaphorical, and highly symbolic; it carries coded religious and political fantasy messages rather than actual predictions, hiding the names of real tyrants behind dramatic substitute images.

Revelation is not journalism! What it communicated was a powerful statement of popular ideas about religious factionalism and a longing for political revolt. The problem comes when a literary vision of the first century is read in later times as if it were factual news reporting.

There have always been, in Judeo-Christian tradition, two distinct streams of thought, one witnessing to a God of love and inclusion, the other to a God of wrath and rejection. In Revelation, wrath wins—ironically, in the name of love—and we see an early form of a sadistic strain in Christian theology that persists to the present time.

The Abominable Fancy

As example, there is the Abominable Fancy, the notion that the blessed in heaven will perch over those who are writhing in hell and delight to watch them, like sadistic birds on a branch. Revelation (Rev 14...) says,

"They shall be tormented with fire and brimstone in the presence of the holy angels, and in the presence of the Lamb: And the smoke of their torment shall ascend up forever and ever...Rejoice over her, thou heaven, and ye holy apostles and prophets; for God hath avenged you."

This idea has been favored by centuries of luminaries, including Augustine, Calvin, and Jonathan Edwards. It was Thomas Aquinas who wrote:

In order that the happiness of the saints may be more delightful to them and that they may render more copious thanks to God for it, they are allowed to see perfectly the sufferings of the damned. (Aquinas)

Clearly, this is a far different perspective from that of lions lying down with lambs, or of loving them that hate you.

WHAT CAME AFTER THE BIBLE

Within three centuries of Jesus' death, differences of interpretation of his teachings and his person had solidified into contentious camps, with sometimes lethal consequences. Traditional Judaism, the old pagan religions, and Greco-Roman religions considered

Christians to be heretics, and slaughtered them by the thousands. Within Christianity differing theologies were in bitter contention, most notably about the relationship between God and Jesus: was Jesus truly divine (of the same substance as God, equal to God) or was he essentially human though a lot like God, with divine qualities? The quarreling was constant, intense, and destabilizing.

Roman Emperors

The military hero Constantine I became Roman Emperor, and wanted an end to the inter-religious warfare. When, in the year 313 CE, he declared Christianity a legal religion, two centuries of persecutions and martyrdom ended just like that. But the internal dissension over Christian theology continued, so in 325 Constantine gathered the bishops of the Church to the Council of Nicaea to decide once and for all which theological position would be considered the correct one.

To put the matter briefly, the bishops eventually voted to accept a statement of faith, the Nicene Creed, favoring the claim that Jesus was divine: "very God of very God, begotten, not made, being of *one substance with the Father*." It is still recited daily at worship services of the liturgical branches of Western Christianity.

Of course, the differences of belief had not disappeared; quarrels continued. But the emperor who followed Constantine I, Theodosius I, believed the Nicene position, and in the year 380 he declared Nicene Christianity the official religion of the Roman Empire. His decree stabilized that theological view as the Western standard and also joined the Church to political power. Both results would mark Western civilization, right up to today.

The decision to declare a single, 'true' version of Christian beliefs did more than make alternative ideas heresies. This was a massively influential turnaround. *Thinking* (beliefs) replaced Jewish emphasis on *living* as the standard of faith. It led, ultimately, to the Inquisition, and to theological tyrannies of all kinds. It also strengthened the concept of dualism; for if only one way of thinking is considered "right," then surely anything else must be "wrong."

Augustine

Into this time of standardizing came the great Augustine—a brilliant theologian with a tormented psyche. In his work we see how doctrine, grown out of Greek intellectualization and Roman focus on beliefs, would completely overtake the Way of Jesus and his early followers.

The line of sadistic moralism in Christianity did not begin with Augustine, but in his work it flourished. His intellect was dazzling, and so powerful that his ideas about sin and punishment and hell became inextricably linked with each other and with sex (about which he was seriously conflicted). Jewish tradition had largely understood the action of Adam and Eve in Eden as an error of immaturity; but Augustine institutionalized it as Original Sin, and hell became serious.

For Augustine, hell was a logical outcome of disobeying God, whose wrath would be, well, God-sized and limitless, a sensory, bodily torture punishing demons and humans alike. In his philosophy, it also became eternal, a punishment of God-like dimensions with no recourse, even for unbaptized infants.

Given Augustine's intellectual force as a theologian, who could say he was wrongheaded? His views became doctrine. Over the next nine hundred years the doctrines would expand and become well-nigh universal, leaving generations of people fearful of their very nature and terrified of a God who seemed to have designed them all for hell.

Dante

And then—the great Italian poet Dante Alighieri provided imaginative descriptions of what hell would be like. It is impossible to overestimate the millions of people who have lived in terror of the specific hell of his *Inferno*.

Dante's description of seven levels of hell is a festival of sins, a showcase of morbid implements of the human imagination. His torments drew from sadistic elements within the deep psyche, inherited from persecutions and embellished by perversions, which would pass on to the Inquisition and other torture chambers. In Dante's words we see an understandable human desire for justice transformed into a pathological vindictiveness, rationalized as vengeance against the Oppressor and sin and projected as an ambition shared by a God of boundless wrath.

Who could have imagined that the gospel of Jesus would lead to this—a brew mixing the logic of dualism and the melodrama of Revelation, stewed in the power of Augustine's institutionalized hell of eternal physical torment without recourse, and Dante's infernal imagery. That hell swept throughout Christendom.

Mistranslation

As the printing press made Bibles more available, and as they began to be published in the vernacular language of ordinary people rather than in Latin, a new problem arose: mistranslation.

Between 1604 and 1611, translators worked to create an official English translation, the King James Version of the Bible. The stunningly beautiful English of their translation has endured and been loved for four hundred years. However, the translators thought in terms of official church doctrine, which means they believed in the Augustine/Dante concept of hell. When they came upon words in the original that meant something different than what they understood to be correct, they overrode them with their late-Christian doctrinal interpretation.

Sheol and Hades

Most damagingly, this affected the words Sheol and Hades, which would accurately have been translated as *grave* or *underworld*. Instead, both they and Gehenna appeared as *hell*. Even though

Jewish scripture has no concept of this hell, the word is used in the KJV Old Testament thirty-one times. The KJV New Testament translates Hades as hell eleven times, and Gehenna as hell twelve times. The overall result is fifty-four references to a hell that does not exist in the original writings.

Tartaros

The book of 2 Peter contains a literary allusion that would make sense to its Greek audience. They would know the mythological tradition about a war in heaven: When the semi-divine giants, the Titans, became rebellious and violent toward humans, Zeus imprisoned them in *Tartaros*, a deep pit far below Hades. The author of 2 Peter uses that story when talking about fallen angels, relating their rebelliousness to the sexual licentiousness and defiance of authority he saw in urban Greek society. He writes that "God did not spare the angels when they sinned, but cast them into Tartaros." *Tartaros* is translated in English Bibles as "hell."

Other vocabulary

Note: The information in this section is available from many sources. The most coherent I found was from Peter Chopelas: *http://churchmotherofgod.org/articles/articles-about-the-orthodox-church/2065-heaven-and-hell-in-the-afterlife-according-to-the-bible.html*

It was not only place names which suffered when translators aligned word choices toward their own doctrinal views. Take, for instance, the meanings of three words from the earliest biblical writings in Greek: *anion, theion, and bazanizo.*

Anion, like our word "eon," means a period of time—long but not endless. It became translated as *eternal, everlasting, forever and ever.* The Jewish and early Christian God punished, but not eternally. It was Augustine who changed it to "forever."

Theion means sulfur. Note its similarity to the Greek *theos*, God; because it is a stone (earth) combined with fire (divinity), it was thought to have divine properties. The stone that burns (*burn stone*, later brimstone) was used in religious rituals as a reminder of God's presence. Burning brimstone was believed to have power to purify and to ward off disease, so it was commonly used to clean and purify rooms, especially in temples, where the association with divinity was natural.

On the other hand, sulfur without oxygenation has a sickening rotten-egg smell. The translators, who did not know the old usages of cleansing, equated *fire and brimstone* to the putrid sulphurous (unoxygenated) odors produced by rotting organic matter earth-quakes, and volcanoes. To the translators, *theion, fire and brimstone* indicated not a sacred presence and purification but the wrath of God.

Bazanizo can be either a noun or verb; it means to try or test gold or silver for purity by rubbing the metal on a black touch-stone and checking the color of the resulting streak. From "test" or "try," the word came to be translated as toil, vex, toss, pain, and most often, torment. For instance, Revelation 14.10-11, which reads, "And the smoke of their torment ascendeth up for ever and ever" would be more accurately translated, "And they will be tested (and purified) for an age and an age' (meaning completely, until it is fully done).

In other words, what the original biblical text intended as a period of correction became *eternal*, the presence of God became *wrath*, and purification became *torture*.

Ten different Hebrew words translated as "punish" do not originally carry that meaning. The word *paqad* simply means "to visit" or "to remember," but is translated 31 times as 'punish.' The word *anash* means "to urge" or "compel" (but is shown 5 times as 'punish'), while *chasak* means "to restrain" (3 times as 'punish'). Such counting is not to be dismissed as nitpicking, because these translation shifts make an enormous difference for Bible readers.

When texts are made more frightening, it not only increases the human cost, but distorts the very nature of God.

PROBLEMS AND QUESTIONS

There are substantial problems beyond hell's being non-scriptural that we don't have time to deal with here, but at least two need mentioning.

Cognitive dissonance

One of the biggest difficulties people of the twenty-first century have with hell is that the concept is cognitively dissonant: People who are even modestly educated about the Hubble universe know too much about geology and astronomy to believe in hell as a tangible place somewhere in the underground of Earth or anywhere in what is known of physical space and time. As philosopher John Hick put it:

> Augustine insists at great length and with many pre-scientific analogies that the damned are embodied and are able to burn everlastingly in literal flames. Of course the idea of bodies burning for ever and continuously suffering third-degree burns without either being consumed or losing consciousness is as scientifically fantastic as it is morally revolting. (*Death & Eternal Life*, 1994)

Some seventeen centuries after Augustine, some details of doctrinal thought truly are too much to believe.

Criminality

Another major sticking point for modern believers is a moral issue. Belief in the traditional view of hell as eternal physical torment for sin of merely human dimensions is disproportionate and inhumane. It not only makes God criminally guilty of abuse but puts God in violation of the Geneva Conventions. No international court would support such incommensurate justice.

SHORT VERSION AND SUMMATION

The notion of a sadistic hell of everlasting physical torment perpetrated by demons and devils has no basis in the Jewish Bible or the teachings of Jesus or Paul, although it has persisted for 1,700 years.

The history of Western religious thought moved from the afterlife as an egalitarian region of the dead, through centuries of human suffering at the hands of other people during which we can trace development of an overwhelming desire for vengeance in an afterlife. This human desire was ultimately projected onto God as the divine plan. By misinterpretation, institutional mandate, and mistranslation people came to believe that this is what Western sacred literature says.

Lack of knowledge of the Jewish Bible (Old Testament) traditions led to poor interpretation and sometimes actual distortion of the biblical message. Mistranslation in both Old and New Testaments substantially shifted meanings; so in the King James Version of the Bible, 54 instances of the word *hell* replace 42 references to a shadowy place of the dead, twelve metaphoric references to impending national destruction, and one pagan mythological reference. Gehenna is routinely translated as *hell*. For four hundred years, readers have been shaped by a skewed version of what the original actually says, far outside the Jewish Bible and the teachings of Jesus and Paul.

THE IRONIC "BUT ..."

Here is the irony: That while denying that hell exists, I have spent so much attention on distressing near-death experiences—*because they do exist.*

There really are (though rarely) visions as bizarre and terrifying as Revelation. Though most NDEs are far simpler, there are deeply disrupting and sometimes hellish ones, as there are closely related lucid nightmares and night terrors, and perceptions of alien abductions—all of them powerful yet none of them readily explainable.

Something *happens.*

We know that something we can call hellish actually exists, if not in a material reality then as experiences in people's lives. But what is it? Is there a universal reality behind these events?

We have no direct access to testable information about the afterlife, because testable data is reserved for the material world; however, just as that limitation has not stopped religious experience and speculation, it does not stop exploration of these puzzling encounters, either. Although we are not able to penetrate the afterlife in a material way with laboratory instruments and measurable data, a different perspective opens when we explore these experiences in their context in this life, this world.

In the medieval religious view of hell, the primary assumptions are that hell is a material place "out there" somewhere, which originates by divine decree (i.e., that torment is imposed by an external force); that what activates hell is an individual's guilt for unapproved behavior or beliefs; and that hellishness involves bodily pain.

But what if the view shifts from an external force to internal? What if our approach to understanding these NDEs does not ignore religious influence but considers an individual's psyche as the source of distress, whether as the avenue through which God works or as a non-theistic mechanism?

In the words of the notable Jungian psychotherapist John Weir Perry, "Stress may cause highly activated mythic images to erupt from the psyche's deepest levels in the form of turbulent visionary experience....and comprehension of these visions can turn the visionary experience into a step in growth or into a disorder perhaps as extreme as an acute psychosis" (Perry, 1998).

This chapter can do no more than point a finger and ask a question. What if hell is not about punishment after death but is about transformation here and now? What if, as Perry claimed, the challenge is "to encounter the death of the familiar self-image and the destruction of the world image to make room for the self-regeneration of them both"?

The question brings us back full circle to the religious theme of apocalypse: turmoil, dissolution, the end of an age. Suffering, death, resurrection. Self-examination, collapse of assumptions, rebuilding.

Apocalypse is psyche, writ large. And so, despite all the micro end-of-the-physical-world predictions across the centuries, and all the *Left Behind* books, the macro apocalypse does not arrive. Consider the possibility that the non-arrival is because the prophecy is not about the world but about the self of the prophet doing the proclaiming. What changes is the individual psyche, the reconstituted perspective that can say the great "Aha!" "Oh, now I understand. Ahh, I get it." And that, properly understood, might change the world.

CHAPTER 9

Is Hell Real?
What Are We, Six?

Confronted by a theological topic, a great many people take on solemnity as the only appropriate tone. Author, blogger, editor John Shore takes a different approach, employing his passion, his intelligence, and a rambunctious sense of humor to make serious points. To some people, his irreverence is shocking; others find him a breath of fresh and healing air. See what you think. **Note**: The post represents Shore's point of view, and its presence here is to suggest nothing more than that I think a good shaking-up is often useful for one's thinking.

This piece is from his Patheos blog, May 24, 2011, and is used by his permission. He writes now at JohnShore.com. John's latest nonfiction book is *UNFAIR: Christians and the LGBT Question* (he is straight). He is co-founder of The Not All Like That (NALT) Christians Project, founder of Unfundamentalist Christians, and has just published a novel.

Asking whether or not hell is real is like asking your teammates in a football huddle whether or not they think it's possible, from your team's current position on the field, to sink a three-point basket.

Wrong question.

Wrong game.

Missing the point.

Here's something I hate: conversations that ostensibly are about answering a question to which, in fact, there *is* no knowable answer. Getting stuck in a conversation like that transmogrifies my medulla oblongata into a crack-snorting hamster on a wheel.

So, to state something so obvious I should be embarrassed to type it: No one has *any idea*—none, zero, zilch, nada, void, total blank — what happens to anyone after they die.

It could be that heaven is awaiting some of us. Or all of us. It could be that hell is waiting for some or all of us. Could be a Dairy Queen awaitin'. Could be a dentist's office. Could be a six-room igloo. Could be interplanetary pinochle tournament.

No. One. Knows. It's. Not. Knowable.

And if at this moment you're inclined to grab your Bible, stop yourself. It's not in there. You can *pretend* the Bible tells you what happens to people after they die, but you wouldn't be fooling even yourself. Paul enjoins us to give up childish things, and you can't *get* more childish than pretending the Bible is a magical window that lets you see beyond life.

Trying to use the Bible as proof of what happens after we die is like trying to use a telescope to row a canoe. [Tweet this.] Wrong instrument. Wrong purpose. Only results in you still haplessly floating about.

The *only* thing we know for sure about what happens to us after we die is that we don't know what happens to us after we die.

I believe God made and sustains this world. So for me the All-Time Great Question on this topic is: *Why* can't we know what happens to us after we die?

Why did God set up this system, in this way? Why *that* colossal mystery?

What is God trying to tell us by so resolutely *not* telling us what happens to us after we die?

If while wandering around the inside of an art museum I come across a door that's solidly locked shut, what do I do? Well, if I'm emotionally immature, I might wrestle with the door's handle, or maybe fall to the floor and try to peer beneath it. I might throw a tantrum because I can't get into that locked room. I might squat beside the door, fold my arms, and determinedly try to imagine everything inside the room. There are all kinds of ways I might waste my time outside that door.

But if mature, I will simply assume that those in charge of the museum know what they're doing, and for whatever reason don't want people going in that room. And that would be good enough for me. So I would turn away from the door, forget about the room, and go back out into the museum, where all those wonderful works of art are waiting to enlighten and inspire me.

I think locking the door between this life, and whatever is on the other side of this life, is God's way of telling us to get our butts back in the museum.

I think keeping the afterlife a complete mystery is God's way of telling us to pay maximum attention to the life we have on *this* side of the door. That the ever-fluid *now* of our lives is where the action is. As clearly as he possibly can, I think he's telling us to with full and focused consciousness *be* in our lives. To love our lives. To *believe* in our lives. To trust that within every single moment of our lives is virtually everything that we could ever want to know.

I refuse to pretend to take seriously the question of whether or not hell is real. I think entertaining the question of what happens in the afterlife is an insult to God and all that he has given us in this life. When we need to know, we'll know.

CHAPTER 10

NDEs, Evangelicals, and the Demotion of Hell

"The New Testament does not describe the torment of Gehenna or portray Satan as the lord of Gehenna. These are later literary accoutrements."

—ANCHOR BIBLE DICTIONARY, S.V

"Theologically, Hell is out of favor now, but it still seems more 'real' to most people than Fairyland or Atlantis or Valhalla or other much-imagined places."

—ALICE K. TURNER, *A HISTORY OF HELL*

Mind you, if you're hoping for a skeptical slam at religion, this post will be a letdown. (My view of Christianity would be nothing like what you would expect, either, but that's a different conversation.) On the other hand, it is fair to ask why, if I don't believe in the medieval description of hell, I keep going on about it. Yawn.

I keep writing about that hell because of the questions in my inbox—because, as the Alice Turner quote above suggests, so many people are living their lives in terror of it. This is especially true of people who have had a distressing NDE type of event and are riven with horror that it might signal that the traditional hell could be true. The group in the worst shape come out of a lifetime in settings where interpretations of Christian doctrine are viciously punitive, suspicious, and fear-burdened (not all Christian teachings are like that, by any means; but these are the ones that get the press).

This chapter is for readers, from whatever background but especially Christian evangelical, who are trying to move beyond a no-exit belief in hell. Even if that does not apply to you and you're an agnostic or atheist, it's worth knowing what it is we're talking about. Feel free to read on.

My intent is to point to some religiously informed and biblically coherent exit signs, ways out of the impasse that is our cultural fear of a particular Christian hell. In brief, here are some online sources I wish I had known about when writing *Dancing Past the Dark*. As an efficient overview of how we got to our ideas of eternal physical torment, these are excellent summaries, much like this book's Chapter 8. Although I am in general agreement with their authors, I do not endorse all their views; nevertheless, the investigation behind these articles is solid and unmistakable even when it is not academic.

From the Winter, 2011 issue of the magazine *Vision* comes "Hell: Origins of an Idea." Brief, well written, and to the point, this article makes the important and usually overlooked observation that it was the turn from Jewish to Greek thought that produced hell as the West came to know it. *http://www.vision.org/visionmedia/origin-of-hell/41044.aspx*

A comprehensive site about the difference between the teachings of Jesus and what became Christianity is *Yeshua before 30 CE*, from which come a number of fascinating pieces including the article "The Church's Development of the Hell Myth." This is a clear and succinct history of the development of Christian thought; in addition, the article builds its case with a wealth of quotes from early sources. *http://30ce.com/developmentofhell.htm*

*"I'll tell you why we must question the teaching of hell.
The very name and character of God is at stake!"*

—JULIE FERWERDER

As clear as those two articles are, they will not meet the need of truly committed Christian Evangelicals who come from a background of a literal and inerrant reading of the Bible. They require more specifics about how it is possible to understand particular Bible verses in a different yet genuinely Christian way. For them a good place to begin is with the highly readable yet thorough book, *Raising Hell: Christianity's Most Controversial Doctrine Put Under Fire.*

Raising Hell is a book as remarkable for the passionate faith of its author as for its scholarship. Issue by issue and proof text by proof text, word by word, Julie Ferwerda, a practicing Evangelical, demonstrates how the evolution of hell across centuries and translations has distorted the Bible's original meaning. Ferwerda's work is an astonishment, to be sure. Again, I do not agree with all her views; yet I think that for Evangelicals, this book may be a life-changer. She asks:

> You may ask, is it safe to challenge over 1,500 years of traditional theology-in-the-making on matters such as whether or not there's validity to the doctrine of hell? …
> I'll tell you why we must question the teaching of hell. The very name and character of God is at stake! What if, by not questioning and not taking the time to get to the bottom of

these matters, we are guilty of completely misrepresenting God's character and intentions to the world? In my opinion, it's not safe to NOT question...

Without a doubt, this book will challenge many core orthodox teachings you've been taught in church, yet my hope is that your Bible will be illuminated like never before. No longer will you have to ignore seemingly contradictory passages or do painful contortions to make the pieces fit... What will change, with perspective, is you.

Superb books are comfortably common these days: any titles by Brian MacLaren, Peter Enns, Rachel Held Evans, and Rob Bell or N.T. Wright can help launch a faithful but new perspective. For a blog, see Richard Beck's *Experimental Theology.* Read their bibliographies for other names. (And if you've heard terrible things about these folks, give them a try. They are people of deep faith, and not a one of them has horns.)

Now that I re-read this chapter, maybe this book is more about religion than I had intended!

CHAPTER 11

Swedenborg's Hell

S ome comments from readers got me thinking about similarities in the ideas of Emanuel Swedenborg (Swedish
scientist and philosopher, 1688-1722) and Carl Jung (Swiss
psychologist and philosopher, 1875-1961). Both were strongly
influenced by their Christian upbringings, and Swedenborg's
visions and writings were directed toward interpreting the Bible
in what he believed to be a more correct way than that offered by
tradition. (It's continually fascinating to me to realize how much
one can discover in the process of challenging one's tradition at
more than the level of adolescent rebellion.)

Anyone with an interest in distressing near-death experiences—any NDEs, actually—really ought to read Swedenborg's
Heaven and Hell. It is available in online versions, handily divided
into paragraph-sized readings. A big plus is its readability.

The similarities between Swedenborg's many visions and
NDEs are so strong that Raymond Moody (1975) devoted a section of *Life After Life* to them, including this description of the
philosopher's idea of hell:

Each person...shapes their own eternity to correspond with
their real inner nature. Some people become irrational,

driven by fear and greed. Such people are in the spiritual condition which Swedenborg called hell…a psychological condition which corresponds to the suffering we experience on Earth when we allow ourselves to be driven by the blind greed of our own egos. There are no devils in hell to inflict punishments because in the hellish spiritual state each person acts out their own malice by tormenting others.

If it seems that without horned devils, Swedenborg describes a tame sort of hell, go look at any of the fifty scariest movies. Or consider what went on in the prison camps of the Shoah (Holocaust), the Inquisition, and Abu Ghraib. Oh, what things our minds can generate entirely on their own, no supernatural devils required!

This ties neatly though perplexingly with a comment from a reader about the Jungian Shadow: "It's the duality of the good we think we are vs. the bad we believe we are NOT—opposites. But it could also go the other way—our Shadow can be something GOOD in us that we are not aware of. Maybe the painful, terrifying NDE is also showing something about us we are not aware of, but need to be. Maybe the positive NDE is too, in some way. Too simplistic a notion, perhaps, or too mechanistic; nevertheless, this kind of experience may not be punishment or reward, but simply a fact of nature" (Personal communication).

CHAPTER 12

Maurice Rawlings and Hellish NDEs

T here's this doctor who's written books about all these hell-ish NDEs. How come he has so many people in hell and other researchers don't hardly at all?"

The doctor was cardiologist Maurice Rawlings in Chattanooga, Tennessee, who between 1978 and 2008 (he died at 87 in 2010) did indeed write almost a half-dozen books warning his readers about the perils of hellish near-death experiences. Here's what I can say with any certainty about why he reported encountering so many distressing experiences.

Rawlings told the story of his patient who collapsed during a stress test, and ,"Before we could stop the machine, he dropped dead." Well, apparently not completely dead, because in the patient's own words,

> "When I came to, Dr. Rawlings was giving me CPR, and he asked me what was the matter, because I was looking so scared. I told him that I had been to hell and I need help! He said to me, 'Keep your hell to yourself, I'm a doctor and I'm trying to save your life, you need a minister for

that.'... And I would fade out every so often, so then he would focus CPR again and bring me back... Whenever I would come back to my body, I kept asking, "Please help me, please help me, I don't want to go back to hell." Soon a nurse named Pam said, "He needs help, do something!" At that time, Dr. Rawlings told me to repeat this short prayer. "I believe Jesus Christ is the Son of God. Jesus, save my soul. Keep me alive. If I die, please keep me out of hell!" (*http://www.freeevangelism.com/testimony/hellandback.htm*).

The experience of the patient, Charles McKaig, then became pleasant, and he reported seeing his deceased mother and stepmother and being surrounded and comforted by the Holy Spirit. Upon awakening, he was an immediate evangelical Christian.

In Rawlings words, "After this was all over, I realized what really happened. It was a double conversion. Not only had this make-believe prayer converted this atheist ... it had also converted this atheist doctor that was working on him"

Years later, Rawlings told his audiences,

"If you can catch people before they die and give them the option of accepting Jesus Christ as their personal savior, then they can't loose [sic] whether they live or die. That is with them forever. And when they die like this, we don't have to question where they went. And the preacher will be right when he says they are in heaven. She went to heaven to be with God. But for those who die on the street, where do they go? It is the minister's fault, your fault and mine because we did not approach them with the Gospel which is the free gift to anyone that wants it."

The website (*http://www.freeevangelism.com/testimony/hellandback.htm*) from which those quotes came has disappeared; but having heard Rawlings speak, I can vouch for their essence. He says similar things in the books themselves (Rawlings, 1978, 1993).

He wanted to get people's attention in order to save them from the hell he believed in. He was giving them a chance to accept a faith he trusted completely. Telling heavenly NDE accounts was not going to win them over; Rawlings was convinced they needed to have the fear of God put into them. He was, in his terms, being loving by being steadfastly and thoroughly evangelical. Essentially, that is the backstory of why Maurice Rawlings reported so many hellish experiences.

Despite the sincerity of his faith, a great many people object strenuously to that fundamentalist Christian point of view and discount his work because of it.

THE SECOND PROBLEM

A different problem underlying the Rawlings material, however, is not theological. The problem, as his fellow cardiologist and fellow Christian evangelical Michael Sabom has pointed out repeatedly, is a distortion of data (Sabom, 1979 and 1996).

A reading of any of Rawlings' books will give the impression that he resuscitated countless near-death experiencers—he himself said that his first book summarized "several hundred" cases and heard their testimonies immediately, and that roughly half of them were "hellish." Sabom's painstaking investigation of the Rawlings data turned up quite a different picture.

Despite what was reported in *Beyond Death's Door*, Sabom found that those "several hundred" cases "were represented by only 21 cases of heavenly NDEs and 12 'hellish' NDEs. Many of these were clearly not from Rawlings' own practice, having been excerpted from other published sources. Others were simply left unidentified."

The same situation presented in *To Hell and Back*, Rawlings' second major book. In a 1996 review in the *Journal of Near-Death*

Studies, Sabom noted that of the thirty-two cases Rawlings claimed, twenty "were clearly lifted and referenced from other sources, and six were personally acquired examples used in his previous books. The remaining six NDEs appear to be new, previously unpublished accounts obtained from his own experience. However, two of these six cases were mentioned only in passing and never described."

In other words, by reusing accounts and padding from other sources, Rawlings was able to give the impression of a far greater number of distressing NDEs than he actually found in his own practice.

Further, his books leave one with the impression that many, many more distressing NDEs would be revealed if only people were interviewed immediately after resuscitation. Sabom's research indicated that conclusion, also, not to be supported by the data.

"In fact," Sabom wrote, "the cases he presents actually seem to favor the opposite conclusion: out of 15 'hellish' cases, ten (67 percent) were clearly shown to have been brought to Rawlings' attention long after the golden 'first few minutes' after resuscitation, four were elicited at an unspecified time, and one 7 percent) was clearly noted as immediate."

There are too many other problems to detail here. The gist of them all is that Rawlings, who was without question a lovely man, sincere in his beliefs and genuine in his concern for people, was working from a highly personal theological agenda more than from a commitment to unbiased information.

What Michael Sabom reported after years of carefully reviewing Rawlings' work was this:

[Rawlings] establishes himself before his audience as a cardiologist with impeccable credentials, a near-death researcher, and a committed Christian. Using these medical, scientific, and religious qualifications, he then presents the NDE as a glimpse of an afterlife and directly applies the Christian doctrine of heaven and hell to these experiences. This gridlike approach, however, poses problems to Rawlings in his interpretation of his and others' research when the type of person (for example, non-Christian) or type of near-death event (for example, suicide attempt) does not jibe with the expected afterlife destination (for example, hell). Rawlings confronts the data of others with authoritative statements substantiated with little or no data of his own and illustrated with anecdotal accounts that, over time, appear to have been altered to fit his own designs…"

Sabom concluded, "I am a Christian and believe in heaven and hell. Based on current knowledge, however, we have much to learn about the NDE, both distressing and pleasant, before we can say confidently just what the experience means and how it fits into our spiritual beliefs."

What this says to us is that before believing any claim about "ultimate truth," or any researcher's sincere pronouncement of having a final explanation about NDEs, it is wise, as Dorothy discovered about the Wizard of Oz, to look behind the curtain to find out who is providing the answers, where they are getting their facts, and what other people of substance are saying about them. This is not cynicism but discernment.

CHAPTER 13

Did Osama bin Laden Have a Hellish NDE?

The news of Osama Bin Laden's death brought a mix of responses, and a couple of people asked me whether I thought he had a hellish NDE. The question brings up some interesting issues.

First, the question suggests belief in "God-as-karma," otherwise known as "People get what they deserve," and points to our looking for a sense of justice. Where does it come from? It seems to be part of the intrinsic human makeup, at least after a rudimentary developmental level.

In individual terms, developmental psychology indicates that somewhere between the ages of three and eight, kids just naturally develop a sense of fairness, as every parent has seen in matters of cookie distribution or equality of sibling discipline. In species developmental terms, the first known, written legal code of any human civilization was developed in Babylon (today's Iraq) about 3750 years ago. In other words, almost 4000 years ago, a king, Hammurabi, defined an elemental sense of justice, a developmental step which was showing up in cultures around the world at the same time. Those ideas also show up in the Torah (Ten

Commandments and assorted elements of law in the Hebrew Bible's Deuteronomy and Leviticus), and in oral traditions in other cultures worldwide.

In fact, the instinct for justice is universal, even across some species. I read a review recently of the book *Wild Justice,* a study showing that mammals have a moral sense: laboratory animals react negatively to unfairness in the distribution of rewards. So, a sense of justice clearly seems to be part of our wiring and no doubt serves a vital role in the survival of relationships in social groups.

On the larger scale, then, in order to maintain civilization, we need there to be fairness, justice. People should get what they have coming, good or bad.

But does wanting the world to be just make it so? No. What works well in building social relationships breaks down in the reality of circumstances in the physical world. Here, peaceful little towns are torn apart at random by tornadoes and landslides, babies and all. Because of political disagreements in high places, innocent families are blasted to smithereens because their homes are bombed. Some individuals spend decades imprisoned for acts they did not commit. Hardworking parents are unable to feed their toddlers while billionaire bosses begrudge them a living wage. On and on, we cry, "Unfair!"

Considering everything bin Laden did to other people, shouldn't we want him (or any dictator) to suffer, even to suffer *forever?* It seems to me helpful to hear what so many people who have had an affirmative near-death experience say about judgment.

What they report defies easy description. Thousands of near-death accounts have been reported in the past three decades, many of them including a life review, a run-through and evaluation of every single thing the experiencers had done in their lives that had hurt or benefitted another living being. During the NDE they not only witnessed their own actions but *experienced their effects.*

In short, the pain and joy a person had given over the years was the pain and joy experienced in the review—what goes around, comes around. God as karma? Without fail, the experiencers report being astonished, deeply moved, stunned by the significance of even small gestures of kindness or cruelty. Now, if the experience of review/judgment can be that powerful for ordinary people, what would it be for a bin Laden? Think of all that pain, that grief and torment he caused! Yeah, he gets hell.

But...

Although experiencers report how vividly they felt the pain they had inflicted, and their regret for it, rarely do they explain it as punishment. Rather, they say, it was more a balancing, an education. The most common response over the years has been a feeling of being overwhelmed by understanding—a life-changing "Oh, now I get it," "I see how it all works," "I see how I could have done things differently." Yes, they feel the pain and their own guilt, but almost always it is less significant than the enormity of the revelation of what life could be—could have been—when lived out of compassion and love.

I have never heard one of these life-review accounts described in terms of a time sequence of punitively imposed eternal suffering (and anyway, in a timeless afterlife, what would be "everlasting"?)

Physician Barbara Rommer, in her book *Blessing in Disguise,* reported hearing from experiencers who had felt judged during their life review; typically, their backgrounds included punitive religious teachings, which some of them associated with the life review. For them, the sense of judgment produced sometimes overwhelming guilt. This only occurred, Rommer said, with distressing NDEs; she did not indicate whether there were disturbing elements other than the guilt.

What matters about these life reviews over all is the frequency of a vengeance-shattering understanding, typically a stunning moment of pain, regret, "getting it," followed by a comprehension turned on its head and a resolve to do better.

To my mind, such life reviews can certainly be understood as metaphors for both the wrath and the love of God, as psychologist

Richard Beck keeps pointing out in his blog, Experimental Theology. To quote his "Wrath of God" post:

> [T]he accounting books of justice are not 'balanced' through a just world, God-as-karma mechanism. Rather, the 'balancing' comes through God *absorbing* the wound of sin, dissipating it in the Divine love… The residual of evil isn't balanced out via karma and just deserts. Rather, it is soaked up in the love of God.

This is a very different perspective from what we hear most frequently. It is also a nearly universal response to a pleasurable NDE.

Overwhelmingly, the great majority of near-death experiencers have maintained that what they discovered in their NDE was a compassion beyond our understanding and a love that can transform all hatreds. Of course it exceeds our human comprehension, and our egos' greedy passion for retribution, and our insistence that God share our characteristics; but surely whatever it is that constitutes the Mind of God must have room for more than vindictiveness. More and more, it seems that we are asked not for vengeance but for transformation.

Maybe bin Laden had a punitively hellish experience, not the life review described by so many NDErs, though I am unsure what of value that would achieve. But I am left wondering, what could be more terrible than to revisit himself and discover so directly the results of his misunderstanding?

CHAPTER 14

Distressing Tibetan NDEs: the Delogs

...[W]hen by the divine messengers
Good people here in this life are warned,
They do not dwell in ignorance,
But practice well the noble Dhamma.

—DEVADŪTA-SUTTA

...If you look inside yourselves there are demons.

—A DELOG

Eastern cultures, as well as the Christian West, reveal similar descriptions of what they take to represent afterlife judgment. In an age of global awareness, these kinds of cross-cultural richness are able to be shared.

A centuries-old Buddhist phenomenon is the *delog*, a Tibetan revenant—a man or woman who has died, traveled through the various realms between life and rebirth and then has reawakened to tell the tale. Some *delogs* make repeated journeys. Their function is not only to make the voyage, but to bring back messages from the dead.

Ithaca College professor Lee Bailey, PhD, writing for the *Journal of Near-Death Studies* (2001), pointed out that the descriptions of after-death delights and trials which make up what we know as *The Tibetan Book of the Dead* (or *Bardo Thodol*) are echoed in the personal histories of the remarkable *delogs,* contemporary and historical

> Seemingly dead for several hours or days, these people revive spontaneously and tell detailed accounts of otherworldly journeys, describing elaborate versions of Buddhist otherworldly landscapes and characters and emphasizing the moral and spiritual teachings of Tibetan Buddhism. These delogs are a bridge between contemporary near-death experiences and ancient shamanic practices.

The *delog* journeys, like NDEs, typically include inexpressibly beautiful landscapes of flowers, sweet fragrances, spiritual masters; there is at least one report of a luminous mansion of light. Unlike contemporary NDEs, they invariably also have a distressing aspect. Note the similarity to the monk's experience as Bailey reports,

> In typical accounts of delogs, as young persons they have been gravely ill and seem to be dead to those grieving around them. But instead, they later report, they had risen up above their bodies, which then they did not recognize as their own. Next these persons' dazed souls enter into a raucous hereafter, guided by their personal deity. They are taken to meet the horrifying Lord of Death himself. They are led on a shocking tour of Hell, where they see numerous condemned souls miserably suffering punishments befitting their sins, such as the nun who hears the unending cries of her own baby whom she murdered. The anguished sinners send urgent messages back to the

living, begging family to do rituals to aid in their salvation and exhorting others to live an ethical life. The astonished travelers meet deceased parents and travel to paradise. Returning to the throne of the Lord of Death, they observe the dreadful judgment of souls with a bridge, a scale, or a mirror. They themselves are judged and given a message to send back. Their consciousnesses return to their bodies on earth. They deliver the various messages and exhort all to practice their Tibetan Buddhist religion faithfully.

One *delog* account from the 17th century included descriptions of terrifying divinities of yellow, red, and green, a bridge over an ocean of fire, and tied-up victims being beaten for having eaten meat. Then she was taken to meet Yama, the terrible Lord of Death.

> Protected by her personal divinity, she entered his palace and trembled as she saw his ugly, red face, wide-eyed and fanged. Wearing a tiger skin, skulls, and flames, he held the fateful mirror of existence, a sword, and water. His frightening voice rumbled like a thousand dragons. He was attended by numerous ugly, animal-headed acolytes and a nasty, little, black demon holding black pebbles signifying the sinful deeds of each poor person to be judged. But a white deity held white pebbles that would weigh against the black deeds. This vast army of beasts was chanting "execute! execute!" or whacking off the heads of the weeping victims.

Just as so many of today's experiencers return with a personal spiritual mission to be lived out in the world, and the NDEs of Plato's Er and the Venerable Bede bring back cautionary messages for the living, so also the *delogs* come back to transmit moral lessons. From a long list of Yama's instructions to a young *delog* come the following, reported by Bailey:

Transmit this message to lamas (spiritual leaders): Let them attempt to be perfect guides for human beings…Transmit this message to government functionaries: do not give without reason illegal punishments, for it is a reason to fall into hell… Transmit this message to the laity: respect your parents, offer food, be sincere, do not beat animals; if you look inside yourselves there are demons. Live so that you will have no shame in my presence.

Whereas in the Western, Augustinian view, hell is eternal physical torment without hope of release, the delog accounts reflect the Hindu and Buddhist doctrines that retributive punishment may be cumulative but it is temporary, and rebirth is certain.

I wrote about *delogs* not to be sensationalist, nor to be critical of shamanic visions in rural Buddhist folklore, nor to say anything about institutional religion. I was not making a post-modern statement about power or human shadow. I wanted simply to say to readers, "Look, here is another group of people having experiences like ours," to have them meet a close relative of Western NDEs, one with similarities and differences, one with an ancient heritage. It is one step on this journey. Make of it what you will.

CHAPTER 15

Images to Shape a Life

We have met the enemy, and he is us.

—WALT KELLY

We spent several months on the *dancingpastthedark* blog—about six of them, in fact—digging around the concept of hell. I pointed out that although the Dante's *Inferno* view of hell is deeply embedded in our culture, it is not biblical. (An observation which is hardly original with me.) I observed that hell does not register as a location on any GPS system. I quoted theological views suggesting that hell may be something other than after-death punishment for bad behavior. It was all very reasonable. As a material presence, hell had been moderately debunked.

But whether we consider hell to be politically incorrect, or simply a concept we despise and run from, or a misbegotten apocalyptic leftover that should be struck out of the language, the fact remains that a sizable number of people continue to experience psychological events that behave very much like what we assume hell might be.

Now what? Where do we go from here?

STANISLAV GROF

The first place I go these days is to the work of psychiatrist Stanislav Grof, M.D., who for fifty years, sometimes in partnership with his wife, Christina Grof, has been exploring non-ordinary states of consciousness which reveal the existence of spiritual dimensions of existence. These are states brought on sometimes by schizophrenia, and more commonly by psychedelic substances or special breathing techniques. Because academic psychiatry had no term for the experiences in this subgroup, he called them *holotropic* (Grof, 1992), meaning "oriented toward wholeness."

He called them that because research suggests that in our ordinary state of consciousness we are able to identify with a mere fragment of who we really are, whereas in holotropic states patients move toward integration of their scattered bits and pieces. As you might guess, holotropic states have a great deal in common, as experiences, with those we are exploring.

HOLOTROPIC STATES OF CONSCIOUSNESS

Over five decades of research and the publication of many books, Grof's studies have built what he refers to as "a useful source of data about the human psyche and the nature of reality."

'The human psyche and the nature of reality'—exactly where we wish to go! Happily, Grof has encapsulated a summary of his half-century of study in a substantial online article, "Psychology of the Future: Lessons from Modern Consciousness Research," from which the quotes below come. You can find the entire article (worthwhile!) by Googling the title or by using the url at the end of this chapter. I also recommend reading at least some of his books.

Defining his term, *holotropic,* Grof says:

> Holotropic states are characterized by a specific transformation of consciousness associated with dramatic perceptual changes

in all sensory areas, intense and often unusual emotions, and profound alterations in the thought processes.

Unlike NDEs, holotropic states may create psychosomatic and behavioral manifestations, and the affected individuals do not typically lose consciousness. On the other hand, NDEs, STEs, and holotropic states all change consciousness in profound and qualitative ways.

> The emotions associated with holotropic states cover a very broad spectrum that extends far beyond the limits of our everyday experience. They range from feelings of ecstatic rapture, heavenly bliss, and 'peace that passeth all understanding' to episodes of abysmal terror, murderous anger, utter despair, consuming guilt, and other forms of unimaginable emotional suffering that matches the descriptions of the tortures of hell in the great religions of the world.

> The content of holotropic states is often spiritual or mystical...Holotropic experiences of this kind are the main source of cosmologies, mythologies, philosophies, and religious systems describing the spiritual nature of the cosmos and of existence. They are the key for understanding the ritual and spiritual life of humanity from shamanism and sacred ceremonies of aboriginal tribes to the great religions of the world.

Remarkably, the holotropic experiences, although seeming to originate in the deeps of the individual psyche, also appear to be tapping "directly, without the mediation of the senses, into sources of information that are clearly far beyond the conventional reach of the individual."

According to mechanistic science, of course, this is nonsense. To the convinced materialist, there is no such thing as 'spiritual' anything, and certainly no 'tapping into sources of information' that even science cannot reach; if science cannot reach it, that information does not exist or is at best spurious. From the materialist perspective we have all been trained into, what exists is the physical universe, and that only.

And yet, based on an increasing body of information, including that of Grof, there is something to be said about some of the mysterious things we clearly perceive to be hanging over the sides of that materialist box—the experiences, odd happenings, gaps, contradictions, events about which at present science has nothing to say. What fifty years of paying close attention has said to Grof is that the patterns of experience he has documented indicate a human ability to "obtain information about the universe in two radically different ways: besides the conventional possibility of learning through sensory perception and analysis and synthesis of the data, we can also find out about various aspects of the world by direct identification with them in a holotropic state of consciousness."

Trained in pre-World War II as a scientist and physician, and after many years of living in the United States academic and medical world, Grof has no illusions about how this perspective will be received by mainstream academia and the scientific community:

> The existence and nature of transpersonal experiences violates some of the most basic assumptions of mechanistic science. They imply such seemingly absurd notions as relativity and the arbitrary nature of all physical boundaries, non-local connections in the universe, communication through unknown means and channels, memory without a material substrate, nonlinearity of time, or consciousness associated with all living organisms, and even inorganic matter. Many transpersonal experiences involve events from the microcosm and the macrocosm, realms that cannot normally be reached by unaided human senses...

And yet again, for all their incomprehensibility and their flying in the face of 'what everybody knows,' some things about these states of consciousness are unmistakable to anyone who has spent any amount of time looking at them:

> Holotropic states tend to engage something like an "inner radar," bringing into consciousness automatically the contents from the unconscious that have the strongest emotional charge, are most psychodynamically relevant at the time, and are available for processing at that particular time.

> ... If they are allowed to run their full course and are properly integrated, they represent a healing mechanism of extraordinary power.

This should speak volumes—perhaps whole libraries!—to anyone who has had a near-death or similar experience. It suggests that what determines the kind of experience one has is not a punitive force, nor the person's character or temperament. nor adherence to the law of attraction or religio-political convictions, but *what is most psychodynamically relevant and available for processing at that particular time!* It is something one is being made aware of, something intensely personal.

As if that were not enough, Grof's analysis is this: that "all that Freudian psychoanalysis has discovered about the human psyche represents at best the exposed part of the iceberg, while vast domains of the unconscious resisted Freud's efforts and remained hidden even for him. Mythologist Joseph Campbell, using his incisive Irish humor, put it very succinctly: 'Freud was fishing, while sitting on a whale.'

And here we are, face to face with the whale.

FACE TO FACE WITH THE WHALE

The first book I read by Stanislav and Christina Grof was *Beyond Death: The Gates of Consciousness* (1980, Thames & Hudson). It is a concise and gorgeously illustrated look at the astonishing similarities in images of death and rebirth across time and a whole sweep of cultures: Christian, Jewish, Moslem, ancient Greek, Persian, Egyptian, East Indian, Tibetan, pre-Columbian, and pre-literate. It was an eye-opener.

Birth, sex, death, and spirituality, as the book illustrates, are intimately interwoven; they have "powerful representations in the human unconscious." In concepts of an afterlife, the recurrent themes and their images are of experiences of endless joy and bliss at one extreme and of punishment and tortures at the other; a journey of the soul may include challenges and obstacles. And far from attracting only negative forces, "deep confrontation with the most frightening and repulsive aspects of human existence can result in a spiritual opening and a qualitatively different way of being in the world."

Whether of bliss or horror, "a shattering encounter with the extremes of human existence has two consequences: 1) a profound existential crisis that forces the individual to question seriously the meaning of human life and reevaluate his/her own system of basic values; and 2) the opening of spiritual areas of the unconscious that are intrinsic parts of human personality structure, independent of racial, cultural, and religious background. The realm of the collective unconscious is therefore archetypal."

The stages of the journey may be represented as concrete encounters or as essentially abstract states of mind. The problem of figurative versus abstract concepts, say the authors, "seems to be less a matter of opinion or interpretation, than a reflection of different types or modes of direct experience of the Beyond." In other words, *the concepts are inherent in the experiences; they are not interpretations papered on afterwards.*

JUNG – COLLECTIVE & ARCHETYPES

The enormity of this is stunning—the scope of the psyche, the living evidence of Jung's 'collective unconscious' with its archetypes vivid in the non-ordinary states of consciousness. But it is not enough to see all this as a really nifty idea, or even a grand concept. It is something else entirely to *feel* the whale breathing in one's own breath.

What Grof has been outlining for half a century is something about the actual structure of the psychological and spiritual universe, made visible in patterns of experiences which illustrate that our waking consciousness is connected to a vast hidden warehouse of images and concepts, the archetypes, shared across time and space. This is all within us as well as beyond us. The archetypes are alive. At the root of the world, the germ cell of the universe, we are interconnected.

> In a large group of transpersonal experiences, the extension of consciousness seems to go beyond the phenomenal world and beyond the space-time continuum as we normally perceive it. Quite common are experiences of encounters with spirits of dead persons or suprahuman spiritual entities. LSD subjects also report numerous visions of archetypal forms, deities and demons – even complex mythological sequences. Intuitive understanding of universal symbols, or the arousal of the inner cosmic energy (Kundalini) and the activation of the centres of the psychic body (chakras) are additional examples in this category. At the extreme, the individual consciousness seems to encompass the totality of existence and identify with the Universal Mind. The ultimate experience appears to be that of the mysterious primordial emptiness and nothingness that contains all of existence in a germinal form, the Void. *[Beyond Death]*

It seems that in our NDEs and spiritually transformative encounters, we have been talking to ourselves, a conversation in which we borrow images from each other and trade abstractions back and forth. As Grof says in *Beyond Death:*

> In the light of recent observations from consciousness research, modern science has had to correct its view of heaven and hell. It is now understood that these are experiential states available under certain circumstances to all human beings...And we have learned that experiences of heaven and hell are of quite regular occurrence when one is facing biological death. The latter fact suggests that we should re-evaluate our attitude toward eschatological mythology. Instead of representing bizarre and ultimately useless pieces of knowledge, the data about the hells and heavens can prove to be invaluable cartographies of strange experiential worlds which each of us will have to enter at some point in the future."

With the related work of Carl Jung and Joseph Campbell, these themes in the work of Stanislav Grof, especially *Beyond Death,* are the best explanations I have encountered
in terms of what is going on with near-death and similar experiences. They normalize what is otherwise, in Western materialism, considered pathological; they constitute what seems to me a believable base on which to begin understanding mythological and religious narratives and images. The book has profoundly shaped my thinking.

CHAPTER 16

The Descent Experience: Struggle & Time

No near-death or other spiritual experience is complete until it has been integrated—incorporated in a meaningful way into its owner's life and understanding. For some individuals, perhaps the process is relatively simple, though I believe it is never that for anyone who recognizes that such an experience not only ventures into an immensity of spirit and cognition but brings something of immensity back to be woven into ordinary everyday consciousness.

As I have said many times, NDEs/STEs do not deal with the doctrines of any particular religion or ideology; those are, relatively speaking, local matters. (But this explains why the experiences kick up such opposition from believers who cannot see the abundant fields lying beyond their personal boundaries.) These experiences go wider than any regional culture and deeper than any conventional wisdom; they deal with an enormity of consciousness.

Into the field of this conviction came a post on the blog *Neurosciece and psi*, of California clinical psychologist Sheila Joshi. It is an extensive essay she wrote with another clinical psychologist,

Barbara Croner, a co-founder of the *International Antidepressant Withdrawal Project*. The essay is titled *"The Descent Experience and the Tertium non datur: Managing the tension and the time of waiting."*

Anyone who deals with the depth of these experiences will see at once why I recommend the Joshi/Croner essay. It is dense enough with ideas and information that reading it may take you some time; but, as the authors point out, the time of processing is part of the endeavor and its result. I think you will find it worth the wait.

The Descent Experience & the Tertium non datur: Managing the tension and the time of waiting

by Barbara Croner & Sheila Joshi

THE DESCENT EXPERIENCE

Since the beginning of time, humanity has described a particular kind of experience that many people have had, but many have not had. It involves terrible suffering. It lasts a very long time. During much of it, there is no help or relief that can be had. Eventually, it draws to an end, culminating in a return to life, often with additional gifts.

It has been called The Descent Experience, and the oldest known recorded version of a descent myth was written by the Sumerians on clay tablets in the third millennium BCE. In this version, the goddess Inanna (also known as Ishtar) has to visit the Underworld. There, she is destroyed physically and psychologically in the most gruesome way. It's bad, no one will help; it goes on for a while. Finally, Enki, the god of wisdom, comes to her rescue in an artful way, deals are made, she is reconstituted, and returns to the world.

Maybe 1000 years later, the ancient Greeks wrote their own descent myth about Persephone, who is abducted, raped, and held captive by Hades, king of the Underworld. It's bad, no one will help; it goes on a while. Finally, her mother Demeter pressures her father Zeus into negotiating her release. Deals are made, she has to spend part of every year in the Underworld, but is allowed to return to the world.

C.G. JUNG – THE RED BOOK

In 2009, the heirs of Carl Jung allowed his account of his descent experience to be published for the first time. Over the course of many years, from about 1914 to 1930, Jung wrote and drew about his own frightening falling apart, during which he confronted the darkness in himself and in the world (including WWI). He wrote and drew in order to save himself. It was bad, there was no help. It went on a long time. Eventually, he found help from beings he encountered in his mind who may have been parts of himself, archetypes, and/or spirits of the dead.

Years later, he said that his most important ideas, the ones he worked on for the rest of his life, and that we remember him for, all came out of this period.

In 1916, still early in his descent experience, Jung wrote a paper entitled "The Transcendent Function," which contained the seeds of some of the most foundational ideas of his life's work.

He introduced the term "transcendent function" to describe a fundamental pattern in human psychology. We are continually confronted with internal conflicts. Initially, he referred to the conflict between the conscious ego and the unconscious, but over the decades this concept has been applied to all kinds of psychological conflicts. Jung believed that these conflicts reflected not only influences from our childhoods, but also a teleological [purposeful] pull toward our wholeness (camilogallardo.com).

When faced with irreconcilable conflict between two needs, the human psyche is designed to create a transcendent third option that never existed before. This creative dynamic, repeated throughout life, leads to ever greater individuation and wholeness. The transcendent function is this process. The product of the transcendent function is called the *tertium non datur.*

Jung borrowed this term -- *tertium non datur* -- from the field of logic in philosophy. It is the Latin translation of a concept attributed to Aristotle, that translates as "the third is not given" (wiki, everything2.com). It refers to situations where there is no logical third option to conflicting propositions, such as "Socrates is mortal. Socrates is not mortal." There is no middle ground. (You may already be imagining how there could be a middle ground!)

In this first 1916 essay, Jung appears to use the term *tertium non datur* in its original sense as meaning that there is no logical third solution to an irreconcilable conflict, while the transcendent function creates something that transcends logic (Jung, Collected Works, Vol. 8, p. 90). However, over the decades the usage of the phrase *tertium non datur* in Jungian circles flipped over to refer, itself, to the magical, third way solution that the transcendent function creates, and that's how we will be using it here.

Waiting: Tension and Time

There are many ills that flesh is heir to, but not all hardships are descent experiences. A descent experience is characterized by a long, long time of waiting while in great tension. During it, it may seem like none of the usual remedies work, or that sorrows come not single spies, but in battalions. Job had a descent experience. Nelson Mandela did. Many chronic illnesses are descent experiences. Neurological damage usually causes a descent experience. Spiritual emergencies are usually a descent experience.

We humans naturally want to be able to *do* something about our suffering. We Americans *expect* to be able to do something about it – and pronto. This long time of tension is, itself, a shocking experience, independent of whatever other suffering each unique descent experience entails. How could nothing work?! Why is there not more help?! What am I doing wrong?! How on Earth could this still be happening?! I don't believe this is still happening...

There are some human experiences that, no matter what you do, require waiting through a long time in great tension.

Why?

Because something is created by this process that would not be created any other way at this time. Theoretically, there is always room for improvement and for doing things more easily in the future. We believe everything in evolving – humans, the Tao / God / mind of the Universe, the laws of physics, the collective unconscious. But, at this given point in time, for this individual, and for her / his role in the Universe, this awful, long time of great tension is what will create what is needed.

Irreconcilable conflict

We humans are complex beings, riddled with conflicting tendencies, conflicting needs. We rarely have one feeling at a time; we have several, some in direct opposition to each other. We don't just have a conscious or unconscious mind; we have both. And so often, we have a desire, but it is opposed or inaccessible in some way.

We humans also experience the universe around us as riddled by conflicting tendencies. Maybe this is just an artifact of our sensory limitations, or our bilateral symmetry, or our being a species that requires two sexes to reproduce. Maybe it's an inherent dynamic of the universe.

As early as 1700 – 1100 BCE, the ancient Indians wrote a religious text called the Rig Veda, which talks about a fundamental cosmic dialectic between the opposing elements of *purusha* (consciousness, masculine, active) and *prakriti* (matter, the physical, nature, feminine, passive) (*http://en.wikipedia.org/wiki/Dialectic,http://en.wikipedia.org/wiki/Rig_Veda,http://en.wikipedia.org/wiki/Samkhya,http://en.wikipedia.org/wiki/Purusha,http://en.wikipedia.org/wiki/Prakriti*).

Around the 6th– 4thc BCE, the ancient Chinese wrote a philosophical text called the Tao Te Ching, which talks about a fundamental cosmic dialectic between the opposing forces of yin (dark, feminine, cold, wet) and yang (light, masculine, heat, dry).

Roughly around this same time – during the intriguing Axial Age when humanity seemed to take a leap in its thinking, spontaneously, across the globe – the Book of Genesis was also produced. It is the first book of the Hebrew and Christian Bibles, and it also talked about a fundamental cosmic dialectic between opposing forces. The first several lines are all about God taking a void and inventing a world by creating contrast: separating heaven from earth, light from darkness, water from dry land, male and female (*http://en.wikipedia.org/wiki/Axial_Age,http://en.wikipedia.org/wiki/Book_of_ Genesis*).

Those are some of the earliest records we have of this line of human thought. Now, we're going to skip ahead to the Western thinker whose name has become synonymous with the dialectic of opposites.

GEORG HEGEL

Georg Wilhelm Friedrich Hegel (1770 – 1831) was a German philosopher who left a legacy of ideas that continues to be influential today.

In recent decades, the classic rendition of Hegel's model of thesis-antithesis-synthesis has undergone some reinterpretation, with some scholars emphasizing that what he really said was abstract-negative-concrete. Either way, he was definitely trying to say something useful about the progression toward greater knowledge. It inevitably involves contradiction, and we should be creative about how we handle those contradictions. In fact, the universe, itself evolves creatively through the relationship between the contradictions.

Hegel scholars also have different views as to whether Hegel proposed to resolve the tension of opposites through synthesis, unification, assimilation, or transcendence. One term Hegel used was the German word *Aufhebung*, which he apparently used for its "contradictory implications of both preserving and changing, and eventually advancement." He also talked about the universe as resolving "being" and "non-being" into "becoming" (*http://en.wikipedia.org/wiki/Georg_Wilhelm_Friedrich_Hegel,http://en.wikipedia.org/wiki/Dialectic,http://en.wikipedia.org/wiki/Aufheben*).

CARL JUNG

A generation or two later, Carl Jung created a brilliant model of the psyche that placed heavy emphasis on the existence and interrelatedness of opposites in mental life. He believed there was no mental energy unless there was a tension of opposites (Dotson, 1996a, 1996b). Some of the opposites he wrote about include: conscious / unconscious, masculine / feminine, Shadow / persona, animal / spiritual, extraversion / introversion, thinking / feeling, sensing / intuiting, causality / teleology (Spencer, nd).

Jung developed the constructs of the transcendent function and *tertium non datur* to understand how the essential conflicts progress. The Jungian analyst and lexicographer Daryl Sharp writes:

"Jung's major contribution to the psychology of conflict was his belief that it had a purpose in terms of the self-regulation of the psyche. If the tension between the opposites can be held in consciousness, then something will happen internally to resolve the conflict. The solution, essentially irrational and unforeseeable, generally appears as a new attitude toward oneself and the outer situation, together with a sense of peace; energy previously locked up in indecision is released and the progression of libido becomes possible" (Sharp, 1991).

The transcendent function is Jung's name for this process, and the *tertium non datur* is the result of the process.

Using the idea of the *tertium non datur* to cope with a descent experience.

A descent experience is profoundly unpleasant, sometimes agonizing. By definition, there are no easy answers. But, it may be possible to get some relief and reassurance from viewing it as a highly productive seedbed for innovative transformation of yourself that would not be likely to occur any other way. Jung gave us a useful roadmap that can make sense of the chaos of a descent experience. It shows how thinking in terms of the transcendent function and *tertium non datur*, and even looking for them more actively, can help us navigate this dark fastness.

TIME

We will now explore why the passage of so much time is unavoidable; why tension (often in the form of pain and fear) is unavoidable; the unpredictability of the *tertium non datur*; some specific implications about neurological damage and psi; some thoughts on the relationship between the *tertium non datur* and the Tao; and, finally, what comes after the arrival of the *tertium non datur*.

Time (often a very long time) is unavoidable.

One of the excruciating characteristics of a descent experience is the unbelievable amount of time it takes. Yet, we ruefully submit that this is the very purpose of a descent experience. The descent experience forces one to wait – none of the usual coping strategies seem to work, and there doesn't seem to be any way to get away from it. If things are going along in a more conventional manner, we have a strong tendency to keep busy and stay distracted, and therefore certain things don't develop. But, when there is great tension over a long time, we are forced to think differently than if things are easy and flowing.

The passage of time is required in order to generate a really new and different creative solution – a *tertium non datur* – that transcends the stuck points in one's life-to-date. Whatever one's personal conflicts are about – self-expression v. loyalty, boldness v. comfort, etc. – holding the forces of opposites for an extended period of time is what brings about evolution. Something brand new is created, something beyond a compromise or settling. Jung wrote:

> "When there is full parity of the opposites, attested by the ego's absolute participation in both, this necessarily leads to a suspension of the will, for the will can no longer operate when every motive has an equally strong countermotive. Since life cannot tolerate a standstill, a damming up of vital energy results, and this would lead to an insupportable condition did not the tension of opposites produce a new, uniting function that transcends them. This function arises quite naturally from the regression of libido caused by the blockage" (Jung, "Definitions," CW6, par. 824, in Sharp, 1991).

A *tertium non datur* only emerges when time goes by, tension builds, and energy is dammed up. Something has to accumulate; there is no shortcut. Think of all the things that require time: many chemical reactions, including cooking our food, or aging wine and cheese. Diamonds. You have to wait for sap to flow. Think of how seeds first go down into the dark, unseen, grow roots, and only then sprout into the sunlight.

Some bamboo will take three years in the ground before any visible growth appears, and then sprout and grow up to four feet in 24 hours (Hancock181).;*http://www.pbs.org/wgbh/nova/lostempires/china/miracle2.html*; http://www.lewisbamboo.com/habits.html)

Even the boiling of water takes time! Andrew Holecek, a Tibetan Buddhist and faculty member at Naropa University compared benefiting from a spiritual practice to waiting for a pot to boil –

> Science speaks about phase transformations, or punctuated equilibrium. A common example is the manner in which water comes to a boil. Put a pot of water on the stove, turn on the heat, and wait. Depending on the intensity of

the heat and the temperature and volume of the water, it will boil slowly or quickly, but either way there is a period when nothing seems to be happening. All the energy is going into the water with no obvious result. The phase transformation from water into steam takes time.

Similarly, when we engage in spiritual practice, we have placed ourselves on the stove and turned on the heat. If our practice is halfhearted, then it takes time for that low temperature to transform us. If we practice wholeheartedly, the higher temperature brings us more rapidly to a boil. Either way there is a period when nothing seems to be happening. Lots of energy is going into our practice, but nothing is cooking.

As long-term practitioners reflect over years of practice, they discover they are starting to get warm. The changes come slowly because the water that is being heated is so cold, and the heart of our practice is usually tepid. But sooner or later we come to a boil. After years of practice we "suddenly" transform from an uptight, aloof person into an open, loving one; from a confused sentient being into an awakened one.

Lasting spiritual changes arise from simply being present, again and again. Religion means to link (ligio) back (re). Linking back on the spiritual path takes place every time we return to our breath, our body, our mantra, or the present moment. With each return we are taking a small step toward enlightenment because being fully present is a fundamental expression of enlightenment (Holocek, 2009).

A descent experience has much in common with any deep spiritual practice, but it is usually more painful and less rewarding for awhile.

There are many things that can't be sped up. Time cannot necessarily be replaced by greater intensity. You can't force a caterpillar to become a butterfly faster. It takes time to get to know who another person really is. You have to wait to see the pattern of their approach to various situations over time.

It is very hard for us to wait in modern Western societies, perhaps hardest of all in the US. There is tremendous cultural pressure to do more and to do it faster. There's something wrong with you if you're not doing a lot, and doing it at the speed of a quantum computer. Descent experiences have always been hard, as the Sumerians told us in the third millennium BCE, but never before have they been so counter to the zeitgeist.

Leave it to the Italians to help us with this problem! There is an Italian musical term, Tempo giusto, that instructs the musician to play the piece at the right tempo. Some interpret this as a strict adherence to the metre, but some interpret it as an invitation for the musician to use personal intuition "to figure out the tempo that the notes in the score imply. In this sense tempo giusto…can only be [found] on a case-by-case basis by examining the overall character of a composition. It is a speed the musician intuits from the structure and nature of the piece itself" (*http://en.wikipedia.org/wiki/Tempo_giusto*).

The Canadian journalist Carl Honoré (2004) has seized upon this infrequently used musical term and borrowed it for his book and mission, *In Praise of Slowness: Challenging the Cult of Speed*, which are about helping us hectic modern people to re-find a more natural and human tempo for living. Painful and coercive as the descent experience is, one of its purposes is to bring us to the *tempo giusto*.

IRONY

There is an irony having to do with the descent experience and time which we wish to mention. During a descent experience, some people find that they are growing, learning, and changing incredibly fast, and yet their overall quality of life – which may involve illness, poverty, imprisonment, war -- remains absolutely stuck. The lack of synchronization between personal effort and internal development on the one hand and external lived reality on the other can be crazy-making and depressing. It will probably be very different from how your life was before the descent experience, when there was much more of a correlation between effort and results.

It is perhaps cold comfort, but still it is true that our experience of time is just one aspect of the whole truth about time. The physicists, parapsychologists, and psi / spiritual experiencers tell us that there is no time, or all time exists now, or the arrow of time can go backwards, or time really can change its pace. But, frankly, one of the hallmarks of a descent experience is that, whatever the heck is happening with time, you're in a bad neighborhood of it.

In the Fall of 2010, Jack Kornfield, Ph.D., psychologist and Buddhist monk, spoke at one of The Red Book Dialogues in San Francisco. In discussing Jung's descent, and descent experiences in general, he said your worst fears are the gateway to your enlightenment. You must face them, you must suffer, yet you must not get lost in the experience either. You stay present to your fears, you wait, you listen. It can take a long time. If you can trust the desert, at some point, it rains. Then, you find out what your gift, your contribution to the world is, "some new extraordinary wholeness appears and that's who you really are."

So, time will eventually be your friend again.

Let us now take up the issue of this fear that Kornfield mentions. Tension (often in the form of pain and fear) is unavoidable.

PAIN AND FEAR

Ah…pain and fear…these are the very worst aspects of a descent experience, but keep reading because we hope to give you some thoughts to help you with them.

As a disclaimer at the beginning, we wish to say that we believe the human trajectory is toward growth with less suffering. There has been a slow shift over the course of human history away from shame, guilt, submission to authority, caste and class assignment, and the general belief that we must and should suffer. There is also an explosion of knowledge and information-sharing going on, in every subject, including psi and communication with Spirit. The Aquarian age will be an advance over the Piscean age in terms of the mitigation of human suffering.

However, at this point in our development as a species, some of us still are going to go through harrowing descent experiences. And to a lesser extent, some tension will probably always be a part of human development.

Tension is inevitable to psychological development.

Throughout his writings, Jung repeatedly refers to tension as an inevitable part of psychological life and development. He thought of the conflict of opposites and the resolution of that conflict as an ongoing aspect of normal development. He called the resolution of that conflict the transcendent function, because he believed it had to transcend logic and reason to be a fully satisfactory resolution. The Jungian lexicographer Daryl Sharp writes: "The transcendent function is essentially an aspect of the self-regulation of the psyche" (Sharp, 1991).

TENSION PARTICULARLY PRESENT IN PURSUING CENTRAL LIFE MISSION

If tension is an inevitable part of psychological life, it is even more present whenever you are working on something that is more central to your purpose in life.

The psychologist and dream specialist Gillian Holloway writes in two excellent blog posts about the relationship between our truest destiny and our deepest fears. She has found in her practice that when people pursue their most compelling mission, they are often beset by their own personal worst fears, almost as if this were by design. She doesn't claim to know why this is, but she encourages us not to back off from our mission, and assures us that the fears are not a sign that we should give up (Holloway,*http://www. flashofspirit.com/blog/2012/09/why-life-purpose-is-so-tricky/*).

Holloway also has observed that developmental steps that increase one's power or one's voice tend to be fraught with obstacles. Again, she adjures us not to take this as a sign that we are on the wrong track.

> Goals associated with power are fraught with challenges the like of which you may never see elsewhere… If your goal will give you more power, even if you are not doing it for the power,expect the process to be filled with weird hazards… These problems are not a sign you should quit. Keep at it and don't let the flying debris hit you in the head. Consider this an initiation or ordeal.

And…

> Goals related to your voice are highly challenging. There is nothing more taboo than your authentic voice. It freaks out the people close to you, and it ticks off the "experts" who should be helping you.

And…

> Be aware of "difficulty at the beginning." There is a Zen principle about "difficulty at the beginning." Very loosely, this translates into finding out that your idea was dumb, not possible, not practical, won't pay, or is not open to people who are not already doing it. This is like a weather pattern that smacks down new ideas. Just realize this is the way of it, not the truth of it. Be rather stubborn about

the "no's" you encounter at the beginning, because they can refine your plan, but should not nullify your intention.

Be aware of "dragons at the gate." When you move toward something that has been a dream of yours, a passionate hope, or something you've worked toward for a long time, monsters will jump out at you from every side, saying you lack the right credentials, "it takes a lot of money," or it simply can't be done! The closer you get to the finish line of your heart's desire, the more dragons will threaten you. This just means you're getting there. Offer the dragons a breath mint and press on!

If you have fears about a project or goal, those fears will be out-pictured in your life. Working on something connected to private fears will magically attract nay-sayers, critics, or technical experts who will pick at you or flatly tell you why it can't be done. Those critics and experts are not signs that you should give up. Instead, they are your fears being "presented" so that you can chose to keep at it. Go ahead and put your thumb to your nose and wiggle the fingers of your hand at them. Then do the next step. This can actually get to be fun. The more something means to you, the more it relates to your voice, your spirit, your purpose, the more fears may be woven around it, and thus, the more silly critics may jump out of the woodwork and say "boo." Don't let them scare you. They are part of the game. Give them your raspberry salute and plunge ahead!

Be willing to let go of the form, but not the essence. The person you loved may flee the scene, but don't give up on love. The job you thought you wanted may be snatched from underneath you, but that doesn't mean you won't be a success. The house you made an offer on may get sold to another, but you still can and will find the perfect home. Separate from the forms when they leave or don't work out, but deepen your connection to the essence. You haven't been told "no," you are simply letting the "not quite right" forms fall away. *http://www.flashofspirit.com/blog/2012/08/are-those-obstacles-a-message/*

These observations of Holloway's are based on 25 years of helping clients and students. She is saying that there is some sort of role for difficulties, for tension, in the unfolding of central life purpose. Tension in the form of fear and pain seems to be an inevitable part of the process.

TENSION IN THE MIDLIFE DEVELOPMENTAL PASSAGE

A descent experience can happen at any stage of life, but it is most likely to happen in midlife. Jung contributed greatly to the understanding of individuation, which is the process of differentiation from others, of developing one's unique personality (Sharp, 1991). Although it is a lifelong project, Jung gave a lot of attention to the big leap of individuation that happens in midlife, which is sometimes very disruptive and distressing.

In an excellent article on the midlife crisis, which incorporates Jungian and astrological concepts, astrologer Candy Hillenbrand writes that the task of midlife is to shift from an identification with ego and persona more towards an identification with one's Self. For our purposes, the Jungian construct of the capital-S Self may be thought of as the greater self that encompasses ego and soul or higher self.

The midlife task also entails incorporating whatever polarities one has not focused on in the first half of life. For example, feminine qualities must be augmented by masculine qualities, and vice versa; creative qualities are to be augmented by analytic ones; introversion by extroversion; etc.

The purpose of this shift to the greater Self and to encompassing one's heretofore less developed capacities is to make it possible to achieve what you really want to do with this life. As you can see, moving toward the less developed polarities in your personality will intensify that tension of opposites that calls upon the transcendent function to produce its *tertium non datur*. You can also see the tension inherent in shifting from ego and persona to greater Self because it involves breaking more than ever with familial and cultural expectations.

Reconciling newly clamoring opposites within yourself and breaking old loyalties often leads to turmoil. As Hillenbrand writes: "...the process involved can be a long and arduous one, and along the path we are likely to encounter all the 'demons' of the past, our deepest fears and insecurities, and in the chaos that can ensue, we may be forced to endure long nights of pain, grief and sadness..." (Hillenbrand, 1997/8).

Although the midlife passage inevitably involves some tension, not all midlife passages are descent experiences. And, again, not all descent experiences happen at midlife. But, many descent experiences do happen around midlife and involve a spiritual awakening.

TENSION IN THE DESCENT EXPERIENCE: CRUCIFIXION

In this section, we have discussed the inevitability of tension in everyday psychological development; in nearing one's central life purpose; and in the midlife developmental passage. Unfortunately, it is still true that tension reaches even more epic proportions in a descent experience. In fact, crucifixion is an apt metaphor for the descent experience, and this archetype is explored beautifully in an exceptional online book (2000-2003) by Ann K. Elliott, the progressive, environmentalist, Jungian, Christian scholar. The book is entitled: *The Christian mysteries as the soul's seven-stage journey to higher ground: Imaged through the pivotal events in the life of Christ according to Jungian psychology, Teilhard de Chardin's evolutionary vision & Sri Aurobindo's Vedic ordering of consciousness.*

Jung believed that in sorting out the dark and light within our natures, and finding our own mature, individuated path, we would all have a psychological / spiritual experience tantamount to crucifixion: "We all have to be 'crucified with Christ,'...suspended in a moral suffering equivalent to veritable crucifixion" (Jung, CW12, 1944/1968).

Elliott agrees that finding one's own center, and daring to separate from the rules and beliefs of others, can be as agonizing as a crucifixion. Shifting from a stronger identification with your ego to a stronger identification with your Self necessitates breaks with family and culture. The cruciform archetype captures this tension between ego and Self, and also the tension between our physical and transpersonal nature.

Elliott writes about the developmental inevitability of agony:

Normally it takes some kind of conflict or pressure to give rise to a new degree of consciousness. Ordinarily this comes about as one "agonizes" or is extremely anxious about something, or concerning which one suffers relentlessly recurring anxiety attacks. The agony of the struggle becomes the crucible in which the new measure of consciousness is separated out and contained. It becomes the empty, hollowed-out place into which God, light, consciousness can enter (Elliott, 2000-3).

AND THE CROSS AS SYMBOL OF THE PSYCHE:

[C]arrying our own cross is a symbol for carrying our own psyche, hence for individuation. Individuation requires us to carry the burden of our personalities and our lives consciously and courageously (Sanford in Elliott, 2000-3).

What it means to embrace the cross:

Psychologically understood, to embrace the cross is to live from the center in obedience to the inner voice of Self and in full acceptance of who one is called to be and what one is called to do (Elliott, 2000-3).

Individuation and the cross:

The discovery of "one's own particular pattern of wholeness" is what Jung intends by individuation. In a spiritual sense, embracing the cross is a matter of accepting one's unique and infinite worth in the eyes of God. In a psychological sense the task is to discover one's innermost creative center and live life from there--not striving to be more or settling for less (Elliott, 2000-3).

The tension between the ego and the Self:

As the work of transformation progresses, the ego's role as the center of consciousness is threatened by the Self's higher authority as the center of the total psyche. As the tension between ego and Self mounts a soul crisis develops which Jung above describes as "a moral suffering equivalent to veritable crucifixion." Just as surely as the Incarnation led to the Crucifixion, so in everyone the tensions inherent between "spirit" and "flesh" become the vertical and horizontal bars of the cross upon which human nature hangs. In the process of the second or spiritual re-birth, the ego must endure the subjective, emotional pain of its own crucifixion.Psychologically defined, crucifixion is the death of the ego's will to rule; while resurrection is the maturation of the transcendent Self whose will is in accordance with the divine will. As crucifixion is the price exacted from the ego and its self-will, so rebirth is the promise of the Self's new transcendent identity (Elliott, 2000-3).

Jung and Elliott also had some interesting things to say about the two thieves who were crucified alongside Jesus. One thief denies any responsibility for his own fate and scorns Jesus, while the other thief takes responsibility for his fate and acknowledges Jesus. It is not entirely clear to us whether Jung thought of the two thieves as symbolizing the light and dark in our nature, or whether he thought of them as symbolizing the ego and the Self, or whether he had both meanings in mind. Either way, he avers that they symbolize an "agonizing suspension between irreconcilable opposites" which, as we now know, he believed would require the transcendent function to resolve and a tertium non datur in order to resolve it (Jung, 1951 / 1959, CW 9, para 79).

Elliott casts the two thieves as the conflict between the ego and the Self with Jesus trying to reconcile the two within himself (Elliott, 2000-2003). Note that the ego is never left behind. It must always exist and be strong. It creates the holding environment for the transcendent function and we need it for everything. Jung stressed that development works better when the conflicts are made conscious and held by the ego: "At this stage it is no longer the unconscious that takes the lead, but the ego" (Jung, CW8, par. 181 in Sharp, 1991).

THE PURPOSES OF EXTREME TENSION

In a simple way, tension is a signal that something needs attention, solution, help, healing, empathy. You would not notice or work on that something if it weren't in tension. But tension is much more than that. It is especially fundamental to creation – the creation of any kind of psychological existence, and the creation of real greatness within us. It seems that there must be some kind of opposition or meeting between two forces for new things to emerge.

Consider the hologram as a metaphor. A hologram is made by taking a coherent light beam, splitting it, reflecting half onto an object and then holographic film, and the other half directly onto the holographic film. The split beam comes back together and creates a 3D image. Perhaps the pure consciousness we are born with has to be split or differentiated in order to again meet itself, know itself, give us new perspectives, evolve and create. We start as pure light, become differentiated, but may lose parts of ourselves along the way, and then have to bring all the parts back together to make a magical 3D version of ourselves.

Jung wrote: "There is no consciousness without discrimination of opposites" (Jung, 1951 / 1959, Psychological Aspects of the Mother Archetype, CW 9i, par. 178 in Sharp 1991).

Furthermore, Jung believed that when you have intolerable, irreconcilable conflicts, that's when something really exceptional is created. "The greater the tension between the pairs of opposites, the greater will be the energy that comes from them" (Jung, On Psychic Energy, CW 8, par. 49).

The struggle makes something different be born than would have been born if there had not been a conflict between irreconcilable differences. The Jungian psychotherapist and actor Camilo Gallardo writes that the transcendent function "unites the opposites for a new attitude to emerge or it can be seen more archetypally as our relationship or interaction with the unknown or other" (camilogallardo.com). And Jungian lexicographer Daryl Sharp adds: "This process requires an ego that can maintain its standpoint in face of the counterposition of the unconscious. Both are of equal value. The confrontation between the two generates a tension charged with energy and creates a living, third essence" (Sharp, 1991).

The tension is a unique experience – it creates a spirituality and a life force of its own during the waiting process. But, in the middle of that process, it can feel like nothing is happening despite great effort, and that you are completely thwarted. There is a paradox – a descent experience creates deep learning experiences about the self, self-love, passions, life-force, life. Yet, during all that learning, you can still be in outer darkness for a very long time. You may think, "What am I doing wrong? Why the hell haven't I found the light? Have I been abandoned?"

In conclusion, what we have been broadly calling tension, but which often comes down to real fear, is a necessary part of the alchemical process. It is essential to the chemical reaction of irreconcilable differences. It's terrible, but it's there for a purpose. Fear and time are essential to the transmutation.

Once you have done everything wholesome you can think of to be safe, healthy, and happy, you must sit with the remaining tension or fear, maybe for a long time, and not short-circuit the process, despite the immense temptation to do so. "Holding the tension between opposites requires patience and a strong ego, otherwise a decision will be made out of desperation. Then the opposites will be constellated even more strongly and the conflict will continue with renewed force" (Sharp, 1991).

But, if you withstand the tension, a *tertium non datur* will emerge, "forcing the energy of the opposites into a common channel. The standstill is overcome and life can flow on with renewed power towards new goals" (Jung, CW 8, par. 827 in Sharp, 1991).

The *tertium non datur* is unpredictable, irrational, and transcendent.

And now for the good news. Certainly, the most enjoyable part of this arduous experience is that the solution to the impasse turns out to be something better than we could ever have expected. Remember we discussed earlier that Jung named it the "transcendent function" because it transcends logic, and the historical roots of the term *tertium non datur* speak explicitly to the fact that there is no logical, expectable resolution to a given conflict.

Not only does the *tertium non datur* transcend logic, it transcends familiar reality. We have only touched lightly on psi, spirituality, and transpersonal psychology in this essay, but let us just mention in passing that Jung thought of the Self as a transpersonal phenomenon, something akin to a soul or higher self. (He, himself, had a very elaborate near death experience, during which he learned a lot about other parts of reality.) So, his use of the term "transcendent function" also referred to his belief that the solution to irreconcilable psychological conflicts entailed something beyond personal psychology and physical reality.

As psychologist Jeffrey Miller writes in his book on the transcendent function: "Though we normally think of the transcendent function as a personal, intrapsychic phenomenon, it is much more. Since psyche is transpersonal, so are the presence and effects of the transcendent function" (Miller, 2004, p. 128).

The *tertium non datur* is unpredictable and unexpected. As far as we can see consciously, our conflict is irreconcilable. There is no solution that we can imagine. So, one of the wonderful hallmarks of the *tertium non datur* is its unexpectedness. As the spiritual novelist Bill Douglas puts it, when his characters must urgently interpret too little information, they had to allow "their minds to fall away from logic and toward deeper patterns, more elegant and complex than linear thought was capable of processing" (Douglas, 2011, p. 318).

Jung wrote:

As a rule it occurs when the analysis has constellated the opposites so powerfully that a union or synthesis of the personality becomes an imperative necessity... [This situation] requires a real solution and necessitates a third thing in which the opposites can unite. Here the logic of the intellect usually fails, for in a logical antithesis there is no third. The "solvent" can only be of an irrational nature. In nature the resolution of opposites is always an energic process..." (Jung, The Conjunction, CW 14, par. 705, in Sharp, 1991).

We have both been in descent experiences for the last few years. While we think it's essential to work consistently at maintaining our lives, and learning, and trying to be more conscious, we have come to recognize that the events – both external and intrapsychic – that seem to be the stepping stones out of the descent are most likely to come from out of the blue and could not have been anticipated despite our keen efforts to do so!

SOME THOUGHTS ON
NEUROLOGICAL DAMAGE AND PSI

One example of a descent experience and irreconcilable conflict with which we are very familiar is that of neurological damage and psi. There is a pandemic of neurological damage and disorder going on due to the Iraq and Afghanistan wars; the creation of new, powerful prescription medications in every category that have neuro-toxic side effects; and the increasing environmental toxic load. We believe that this surge in neurological vulnerability is being enlisted by Gaia and the Tao as an opportunity to jump start a widespread reconnection with our innate psi.

Psi, the ability to know and affect things across time and space beyond the reach of our senses and body, has been pushed into the collective and individual unconscious for millennia. Now, it takes great effort for most people to re-integrate it into their conscious experience. Yet, it is our normal birthright, and to live without it is to live artificially constrained. And, some people think we cannot afford to be artificially constrained if we are to salvage life on Earth. Biologist Lyall Watson: "As man uses up the resources of the world, he is going to have to rely more and more on his own. Many of these are at the moment concealed in the occult – a word that simply means 'secret knowledge' and is a very good description of something we have known all along but have been hiding from ourselves" (Watson, 1973, p. xi). And psychiatrist Stanislav Grof: "A radical inner transformation and rise to a new level of consciousness might be the only real hope we have in the current global crisis brought on by the dominance of the Western mechanistic paradigm" (Grof in Peirce, 2009, p. xx).

Neurological damage often creates a descent experience. A descent caused by neurological damage may be thought of a particular type of distressing spiritually transformative experience. As was mentioned earlier in Ann Elliott's discussion of the crucifixion archetype, tension between our physical nature and our spiritual nature / consciousness is a classic developmental duel, but in the case of neurological damage, that tension has reached catastrophic proportions.

In the field of parapsychology, neurological incidents have long been anecdotally linked to psi openings. We are still in the preliminary stage of understanding why this is.

One way to look at the relationship between neurological damage and psi is that they are in irreconcilable conflict with each other, and require the transcendent function to arrive at a *tertium non datur*. "Being very psychic," or, more accurately, "being very conscious of psi and integrating it into your life to a highly developed degree" seems to be on the opposite end of the spectrum of human health and prowess from having "brain damage."

Yet we assume that both are present at the same time in cases of neurological damage, since we subscribe to James Carpenter's First Sight model and believe that psi is an inherent, foundational way that we interact with reality all the time. It just tends to be unconscious and unrefined in most of us.

So you have a person who is experiencing the profound physical, cognitive, and emotional dislocation of neurological damage and recovery, who is also automatically equipped to draw information from any place and any time and to affect matters beyond physical reach, but they either don't know this at all, or are only beginning to suspect it, or believe it, but still can't make it operate very well.

How do you move through this ironic paradox, this thwarting impasse? You "work your steps," as they say in the recovery community, with exercise, study, healing practices, etc. This is all helpful and expediting, but the tension must still be borne for some time. At long last, a *tertium non datur* will arise that never could have been anticipated.

Laura Bruno, the TBI [traumatic brain injury] survivor and medical intuitive is a good example of this. After a car accident, she had debilitating neurological damage, and mostly had to sit or lie and do nothing for the first year or so of recovery. Among other symptoms, she had pernicious migraines. At some point, she started having sudden, unsought, accurate intuitions about the medical conditions of others. She found that the migraines would grow worse if she kept the intuitions to herself, and the migraines would abate if she told the intuition to the intended recipient. She went on to heal fully, and change career paths from English Lit academic to medical intuitive – something which never would have crossed her mind before the neurological accident (*http:// neuroscienceandpsi.blogspot.com/2012/04/laura-bruno-tbi-survi- vor-medical.html*).

Some thoughts on the Tao and the *tertium non datur*

In this essay, we have focused on a particular kind of human experience, but Jung did state that the transcendent function and its resulting *tertium non datur* are integral to all psychological development all throughout life. The magical quality of the *tertium non datur* just becomes even more evident when the human condition is more severe.

Likewise, the transcendent function and resulting *tertium non datur* are characteristic of how the Tao works. But when the *tertium non datur* has a particularly impressive quality, you get the sense that you are seeing the workings of the Tao more clearly than usual.

We humans are still groping to understand whether the Tao or God or the mind of the universe exists, how it works, and how best to work with it. But, there have been many different streams of thought that suggest that there is intelligence, plan, and order, and that we do best when we try to discern that and align ourselves with it.

We are talking about creation here. You find yourself at an impasse. You've tried everything you can think of. You desperately need a solution, yet you have none. You have nothing. It is out of the nothingness that the *tertium non datur* eventually emerges, as if something were created in the zero point field of infinite, unformed, untapped potential.

Unexpected, elegant solutions from out of the blue are the hallmark of how the Tao works. The Tao seems to be particularly associated with *tertium non datur*s -- taking irreconcilable conflicts and co-creating with you a third, brand new way.

David Sunfellow, founder of NewHeavenNew Earth, wrote:

> Finally, while classic enlightenment experiences lead one to believe that there is nothing new under the sun — that the Ground of Being is all there really is and It is eternal and unchanging — I've also come to believe that brand new experiences, on all levels, are actually unfolding as we (and the created universe) evolve. While this is plainly obvious on the physical level, I think it is also true on the spiritual level (Sunfellow, 2011, http://nhne-pulse.org/the-purpose-of-life-jesus-ndes/).

In order to create something really new for you, and perhaps new for others as well, you have to be open to the unknown. You have to hold the tension (aka fear) and the time. With age and experience you get better at this, and better at keeping a lookout for the *tertium non datur*.

One of the reasons the *tertium non datur* is so enigmatic and hard to anticipate is that it reconciles parts of the self that are more conscious with parts that are less conscious. The less conscious parts include the greater Self or soul and the Shadow or parts of ourselves we feel uncomfortable with (which can be both "negative" and "positive"). With age and experience, we also get better at knowing and holding these different parts of ourselves.

Indeed, this is the quintessential human struggle – the struggle to be who we're really supposed to be, and not just who we might have thought we were. And key to finding / making deeper meaning in our lives is being able to go through all the paradoxes, contradictions, and conflicts of our inner and outer worlds. The *tertium non datur* specializes in navigating paradox.

Furthermore, by going through a lot of encounters with the *tertium non datur*, you become more of a co-creator with the universe. You learn better how to dance with the Tao, when to lead and when to follow, when to try hard and when to surrender. You even come to expect the unexpected.

THE *ASCENT* EXPERIENCE AND THE SPIRAL

Descent experiences come to an end. If you are in one as you read this, they really do. We have read countless stories of descent experiences, and the similarities are so striking, regardless of the cause. People often report a period of "ascent" when things have started to change for the better, but are still hard, followed by arrival at a new stage of their lives where they are astounded to encounter an unprecedented peace and ease.

Katabasis is the ancient Greek word for a descent, and *anabasis* is the ascent. The oldest myths of descent always lead to an ascent to a new life.

Ann K. Elliott, the Jungian Christian scholar, writes about the ascension that follows crucifixion and descent. She notes that in the Bible, in Jungian theory, and in her own dreams, spirals and spinning movement appear as symbols of ascension (Elliott, 2000-3).

Jungian Analyst Martha Blake also notes that many different ancient traditions speak of a primal spiral creative force, and furthermore characterize it as feminine. Interestingly, she writes that the ancient Greek natural philosopher Anaxagoras hypothesized that order was brought out of original chaos by a rotational force and by the interaction of opposites (Blake, *http://www.marthablake. com/tornado.html*). You can see how this jibes with the transcendent function and the *tertium non datur*.

Blake goes on to cite Jungian Analyst Neil Russack as having written that: "Spirals may signify equilibrium in a state of disequilibrium, the stability of being contained in the womb of change, growth that retains ultimate shape, and thus permanence despite its asymmetry." And Blake quotes Jung: "The spiral in psychology means that when you make a spiral you always come over the same point where you have been before, but never really the same, it is above or below, inside, outside, so it means growth."

Spiraling, rotating movement is apparent at all levels of the physical universe. (See section on "spin" here http://neuroscienceandpsi. blogspot.com/2012/06/interview-with-rosalyn-bruyere.html).

In a seminar given in the 1930s, while discussing a dream, Jung explains:

> Dr. Jung: Yes, and moreover, the very symbol of unfolding and the beginning of development follows the law of the spiral: a plant grows in a spiral, and the buds or the beginnings of leaves are arranged in a spiral. It is, as Dr. Barker points out, the functioning of opposites, the reconciliation of opposites. The man who discovered the mathematical law of the spiral [Jacob Bernoulli] is buried in my native town, Basel, and on his tombstone a spiral is carved with this very significant and beautiful inscription: "eadem mutata resergo," which means, literally translated: in an identical way, changed, I lift myself up. It is a circular movement with a slight lift which produces the spiral.
>
> Dr. Baynes: Is it the reconciliation of the idea of change and the idea of sameness?

Dr. Jung: Exactly. The spiral moves away from the original place to another, yet it always returns to the same place, but just a fraction above; always moving away and always coming to the same. Sameness, non-sameness. So the spiral is really a very apt symbol to express development. You see, this vision says: if you surrender to the terror of the blood, you will discover that it leads to development; instead of leading down into hell, it leads upwards (Jung, Douglas, & Foote, 1997, p. 243).

THE FOURTH PROTOCOL

Finally, after a period of ascension, we arrive a new stage of life, a new level of stable identity. After tolerating irreconcilable conflict, and after achieving the transcendent third, we arrive at a state of integration and stability.

Jung observed this progression, and used an alchemical metaphor to capture it. The "Axiom of Maria" is an alchemical principle attributed to an early woman alchemist that: "One becomes two, two becomes three, and out of the third comes the one as the fourth." Jungian Analyst Lara Newton writes that this precept "speaks of the alchemical procedures which unite and separate, procedures that are to be performed again and again to the same substance (using the sun, using divine water, using sulphur or mercury) — each time the procedure is followed brings us closer to the state of perfection that all alchemists seek" (Newton, 2012).

According to the Jungian Analyst and lexicographer Daryl Sharp:

Jung used the axiom of Maria as a metaphor for the whole process of individuation. One is the original state of unconscious wholeness; two signifies the conflict between opposites; three points to a potential resolution; the third is the transcendent function; and the one as the fourth is a transformed state of consciousness, relatively whole and at peace" (Sharp, 1991).

As an illustration of this model, Jung had a fascinating critique of the Christian trinity of Father, Son, and Holy Spirit. He saw it as being incomplete until it incorporated the feminine and chthonic principles as well, and thus became a quaternity. Not surprisingly, he believed that true psychological health required the acceptance of the underworld, Shadow, evil, or Satan in all of us. And, as for the importance of the feminine (and masculine) for everyone, he actually wrote a letter of congratulation to Pope Pius XII in 1950 when the Catholic Church officially proclaimed that the Blessed Virgin Mary had been assumed bodily into heaven, thus adding the feminine principle to the Trinity (Brabazon, 2002; ttp://en.wikipedia.org/wiki/Jungian_interpretation_of_religion).

Mary may have been taken up into heaven, but for us the fourth, the quaternity, speaks to reaching a little bit of heaven here on Earth. It stands for the archetypal human experience of arrival at a longed-for destination of wholeness and peace. It's a reminder that this is possible and that it happens and that other humans have described it. If you are not in such a place now, if you never have been, it is hard to believe this is not pie in the sky. Certainly, one does not ever stop growing, learning, evolving, maturing, so life does not become static and unchanging at some point. But there is an enormous variety of human experience, and one of the things that is possible is to feel "arrived," and this is what descent experiences are designed *for*.

SOURCES

Brabazon, M. (2002). Carl Jung and the trinitarian self. Quodlibet Journal, v. 4, n. 2-3.http://www.quodlibet.net/articles/brabazon-jung.shtml

Deerfield Beach, Florida: Health Communications, Inc.

Dotson, M.L. (1996a). Jung and Heraclitus.http://members.core. com/~ascensus/docs/jung2.html

Dotson, M.L. (1996b). Jung and alchemy.http://members.core. com/~ascensus/docs/jung3.html

Douglas, B. (2001). Conspiracy of spirits: Wall Street vs. the 99%. Illumination Corporation Publishing.

Elliott, A.K. (2000-2003). The Christian mysteries as the soul's seven-stage journey to higher ground: Imaged through the pivotal events in the life of Christ according to Jungian psychology, Teilhard de Chardin's evolutionary vision & Sri Aurobindo's Vedic ordering of consciousness.Online book. Cited here: The crucifixion. *http://murraycreek.net/higher/chapter4.htm* The ascension. http://murraycreek.net/higher/chapter7.htm

Gallardo, C. (nd). The mechanics of the transcendent function.http:// www.camilogallardo.com/index.php

Hancock, M. (2011). The medium next door: Adventures of a real-life ghost whisperer.

Hillenbrand, C. (1997 & 1998). The quest for soul at midlife. Federation of Australian Astrologers Journal, 28. http://www. aplaceinspace.net/Pages/CandyMidlife.html

Holloway, G. (5 Aug 2012). Obstacles: Message or challenge?http://www.flashofspirit.com/blog/2012/08/ are-those-obstacles-a-message/

Holloway, G. (19 Sep 2012). Why life purpose is so tricky?*http://www. flashofspirit.com/blog/2012/09/why-life-purpose-is-so-tricky/*

Holocek, A. (2009). The power and the pain: Transforming spiritual hardship into joy. Ithaca:Snow Lion Press. (Excerpted from the Autumn 2010 issue of Light of Consciousness by Utne Reader http://www.utne.com/mind-body/Cultivating-Spiritual-Life-Practice-Repetition.aspx)

Honoré, C. (2004). In Praise of Slowness: Challenging the Cult of Speed. San Francisco: HarperSanFrancisco. (Available on DVD, too, from Sounds True.)

Jung, C.G. (1951 / 1959) Aion: Researches into the phenomenology of the Self. Collected Works Vol 9, 2nded. London: Routledge.

Jung, C.G. (1944 / 1968). Psychology and alchemy. Collected Works Vol. 12, 2nded. London:Routledge.

Jung, C.G., Douglas, C., & Foote, M. (1997). Visions: Notes on the seminar given given in 1930-1934, Vol. 1. Princeton: Princeton University Press.

Miller, J.C. (2004). The Transcendent Function: Jung's Model of Psychological Growth Through Dialogue With the Unconscious. Albany, NY: SUNY Press.

Newton, L. (2012). My first blog post – thoughts on the Axiom of Maria.http://www.laranewton.com/my-first-blog-post/

Peirce, P. (2009). Frequency: The power of personal vibration. New York: Simon & Schuster.

Sharp, D. (1991). Jung lexicon: A primer of terms and concepts.*http://www.psychceu.com/jung/sharplexicon.html*

Spencer, W.B. (nd). Carl Jung. *http://castle.eiu.edu/psych/spencer/Jung.html*

Sunfellow, D. (2011). The purpose of life, Jesus, and NDEs. http://nhne-pulse.org/the-purpose-of-life-jesus-ndes/

Watson, L. (1973). Supernature: A natural history of the supernatural. Aylesbury, UK: Coronet Books.
http://en.wikipedia.org/wiki/Law_of_excluded_middle
http://everything2.com/title/Tertium+non+datur

http://en.wikipedia.org/wiki/Dialectic
http://en.wikipedia.org/wiki/Rig_Veda
http://en.wikipedia.org/wiki/Samkhya
http://en.wikipedia.org/wiki/Purusha
http://en.wikipedia.org/wiki/Prakriti
http://en.wikipedia.org/wiki/Daode_jing
http://en.wikipedia.org/wiki/Yin-yang
http://en.wikipedia.org/wiki/Axial_Age
http://en.wikipedia.org/wiki/Book_of_Genesis
http://en.wikipedia.org/wiki/Georg_Wilhelm_Friedrich_Hegel
http://en.wikipedia.org/wiki/Aufheben
http://laraowen.com/articles/astrology-as-a-tertium-non-datur/
http://www.pbs.org/wgbh/nova/lostempires/china/miracle2.html
http://www.lewisbamboo.com/habits.html
http://en.wikipedia.org/wiki/Tempo_giusto

PART III

PATTERNS

CHAPTER 17

Patterns and Sasquatch

DEVELOPMENT

Blake Island State Park sits enviably in the middle of Puget Sound, a cruise boat ride out of Seattle. Thickly forested, in warm months the small island is home to Tillicum Village, a popular tourist destination of (or at least about) the First Nation peoples of the Pacific Northwest. There, after a Pacific Northwest meal of salmon cooked over an alder-wood fire, visitors can watch as a dance troupe performs a telling of the Sasquatch legend, weaving it through the edge of the Douglas fir forest. There, just inside the forest, an elusive dark beast, shadowed and not quite identifiable, appears, vanishes, then reappears among the great trees. The mysterious creature is both there and not-there, real but never quite graspable.

For me, as a veteran of a deeply disorienting NDE, the image provided a powerful and freeing sense of a nameless truth that is the archetypal ground of my Void experience: both there and not-there, real but never graspable. It's a lot like hunting Sasquatch, this intense business of parsing distressing near-death experiences. At the blog, we covered a lot of ground, getting glimpses of something before once again seeing the quarry lumbering off into denser woods just ahead.

For a while in the previous chapter, 'The Descent Experience,' I was seeing flickers of comprehension and hints of correspondences—thank you, Sheila Joshi and Barbara Croner!—but then I lost the trail and only later stumbled onto it again. On my umpteenth reading of their essay, certain words jumped out from what they were saying about a fundamental pattern in our psychology:

"We are *continually* confronted with internal conflicts... Jung believed that these conflicts reflected not only influences from our childhoods, but also a teleological [purposeful] pull toward our wholeness.

"When faced with irreconcilable conflict between two needs, the human psyche is designed to *create* a transcendent third option *that never existed before.* This creative dynamic, *repeated throughout life,* leads to *ever greater* individuation and wholeness."

What occurred to me is this: that *it is the conflicts that pull us toward our wholeness.* And those recurring conflicts happen over time. It is not all at once. The "pull toward our wholeness" is *developmental.*

For some time now I have been wanting to talk about developmental stages because of their impact on how we understand distressing NDEs. (Actually, they direct our interpretation of life itself, but this is a book, not an encyclopedia)

"Development" in this sense means the changes, typically age-related, that mark a human lifetime. We begin as infants and continue until our death to move through periods marked by recognizable, generally age-related behavior patterns and capacities. We are all familiar with the idea of physical development, but abundant research has also revealed stages of cognitive development, and emotional, social, moral, and faith development also, that can be tracked throughout life.

Whether of cognition, faith, or any other category, recognizable stages appear sequentially, always building on what went before. They are less linear than spiral. Their direction is toward expansion of boundaries, moving toward greater inclusiveness, not in straight lines but curving back and forth from older stages toward expanded levels that take in wider perspectives. As with any hatching, the transition from one stage to the next is anticipated and accompanied by discomfort and conflict.

Of all the developmental stage theorists, the most pertinent for studies of near-death experience is James Fowler, author of the seminal *Stages of Faith: The Psychology of Human Development and the Search for Meaning.*

STAGES OF FAITH

In Fowler's terms, a clear announcement on the dust jacket of the book announces his topic: "Faith...is not necessarily religious, nor is it to be equated with belief. Rather, faith is a person's way of leaning into and making sense of life. More verb that noun, faith is the dynamic system of images, values, and commitments that guide one's life. It is thus universal: everyone who chooses to go on living operates by some basic faith." (1981)

Over a lifetime of research, much of it at Emory University, Fowler identified six stages of faith. The stages are identified by an individual's perception of authority and the sophistication of his/her understanding of symbolism. Further, in all six stages (and a theorized seventh) what is important is not the specific beliefs which describe that faith but how the person cognitively processes its symbols and myths. *What develops is the way of thinking, not the content.*

Because the stages involve patterns of thinking rather than the actual content of beliefs; they are consistent, regardless of whether the developing faith is religious or secular (for example, Marxism, capitalism, scientism, nationalism).

Stage 0. Primal faith. This is the "landing platform," infancy - age 2. Soaking in the environment: What is it like in this place?

Einstein's question: "Is the universe friendly?" Is the environment warm, safe, caring, or isolating, painful, rejecting; the answer establishes the foundation of trust or mistrust on which all subsequent faith will be built. Relationally, mother as the earliest foundation for relationship with the divine.

Stage I. Preparation. Intuitive-Projective faith. Age 3 - 7. Major achievements: becoming aware of self as a separate creature and discovering language. Egocentric. Soaking-in of stories, images, cultural customs, and taboos. Openness to the Unconscious, strongly imaginative mix of fantasy and reality; much play-acting; powerful and long-lasting experiences and images. Logic is rudimentary. Morality based on obedience, fear of punishment.

Trigger of transition to next stage: emergence of the important ability to be logical about concrete and specific things—for instance, a tall, thin glass and a short, fat glass may hold the same amount of milk—known as concrete operational thinking.

Stage 2. Accepting a specific 'box' of faith. Mythic-Literal faith. Main achievement: concrete operational thinking, but not yet able to work with abstract ideas. Elementary-middle school, although some adults remain here throughout life.

Accepts whatever authority says; takes in the stories told them by their community in very literal ways. Cosmic stories ("Where did the world come from?") are anthropomorphic. Unable to step back from stories to formulate reflective, conceptual meanings; only the literal level exists. Strong belief in justice, reciprocity: black or white, you're in or you're out, eye for an eye: "You scratch my back, I'll scratch yours," "I do what God wants, so God will be good to me."

Triggers for transition to Stage 3 include conflicts and contradictions in authoritative stories, as ability grows to reflect on meanings (realness of Tooth Fairy, Genesis creation versus evolution); breakdown of literalism; disillusionment with teachers and teachings.

Stage 3. Blind faith; inside the box. Synthetic-Conventional faith. Begins late middle school and adolescence and is the most common adult stage. Interpersonal and conformist. Primary achievement: a sense of personal identity as part of the system. Authority is external, residing in traditional roles or in the trusted group. Relational: God as Friend, Companion, Judge; a personal reality. Synthetic in the sense of pulling things together; doubts and questions are dangerous. The Stage 3 individual lives inside of an ideological box, deeply feeling values and beliefs but with no recognition that there is a box. Group's perspective is taken for granted as "what everybody says." Differences of outlook with others are experienced as differences in "kind" of person. Symbols are tied to meanings: to some religious persons, an astrological sign may be seen as carrying the power of evil forces; to a patriot, casual treatment of a revered symbol such as the flag is viewed as blasphemy toward what the symbol represents. The most common stage of adult faith.

Triggers to transition include: the rise of doubts and clashes with authority sources and interpretations; questioning policies previously considered untouchable; leaving home or otherwise encountering differing perspectives that lead to reflection on how beliefs and values are relative to a particular group or background.

Stage 4. Questioning. Individuative-Reflective faith. Typical in young adulthood, but many adults never move to this stage. Recognition and questioning of the box. Discovery that there are other boxes outside it. The questioning and demythologizing stage; sees contradictions, challenges previous interpretations of beliefs, translates symbols into conceptual meanings (flattening connotations into denotations). Concerned with boundaries, authenticity. Assuming responsibility and authority for oneself rather than through the group. Law and order orientation, emphasis on rules and duties, logic, rationality. Viewed from stages 2 or 3, Stage 4 people seem to be backsliding, losing faith, when they are actually moving ahead.

Triggers to transition to next level: What may feel like anarchic inner voices or heresies disrupt the 'law and order' of Stage 4 conceptions; disillusionment with logical compromises; recognition that life is more complex than can be comprehended by clear distinctions and abstract concepts.

Stage 5. Out of the box. Conjunctive faith. Unusual before mid-life, if then. Softens and makes more permeable everything Stage 4 tried to make clear and distinct. Complex, non-literal understanding of truths in stories and symbols; openness to wisdom from diverse traditions. Return to myths and sacred stories, but without being stuck in an ideological box. Sees levels of meaning simultaneously, finds sole reliance on logic and ideological consistency limiting. Symbols are now understood for their underlying power rather than surface literalism: "the second naïveté." Tolerant of ambiguity, paradox, recognition of truth as partial. Social contract orientation, looking to the good of all. Often mystical, living with a constant awareness of the transcendent. Stage 5 "lives and acts between an untransformed world and a transforming vision and loyalties" (Fowler).

Stage 6. Universalizing faith is exceedingly rare. Beyond the boxes. The rare persons who may be described by this stage are said to have a special grace that makes them seem more lucid, more simple, and yet somehow more fully human than the rest of us: Jesus, Gandhi, Malcolm X, Mother Theresa, Martin Luther King, Jr. (Fowler). The element that Stage 6 persons have in common is that they are driven by a vision of justice for all humanity so compelling that it supersedes normal boundaries.

"Universalizers are often experienced as subversive of the structures (including religious structures) by which we sustain our individual and corporate survival, security and significance, and frequently die at the hands of those whom they try to change. They are often more honored and revered after death than during their lives. The essential difference between Stage 6 and Stage 5 is that the commitment to one's vision becomes complete."

You might like to take a look at two really useful charts summarizing two strands of developmental stage theory.

http://www.usefulcharts.com/psychology/james-fowler-stages-of-faith.html

http://www.usefulcharts.com/psychology/kohlberg-stages-of-moral-development.html

THE WD-40 OF STAGE THEORY

Knowing about developmental stages is not a way to cast the world into concrete-like descriptive blocks, but—a lot like knowing about street signs or Myers-Briggs personality types—it contributes to knowing where we are, to making human differences more easily fathomable.

A displeased evangelical letter-writer asks rhetorically: "Do near-death experiences fall under the category of man trusting in himself instead of God? Yes! Why? Because near-death experiences contradict Scripture!"

Reading that, I can be certain that the writer is functioning at one of the less nuanced stages of understanding faith, at a literal level. Before responding, I can recognize that this person will consider only a voice from his vision of Scripture as being valid. A discussion based on our personal views will not satisfy either of us. If I am able to reply in terms that reflect the values he respects, we may have something to say to each other.

From a militantly atheistic faith stance at that same level of inflexibility, there is this: "Why would we care about a perspective that is based on false assumptions? I do feel justified in placing judgments on people who believe things which are unsupported by evidence... I actually expect them to recognize that their beliefs are unsupported by the evidence and that they should recognize them as silly." Blind faith here, with little chance of real conversation. Maybe say something mildly hopeful about new discoveries, and move on.

A person from either of those backgrounds will have a painful time coming to terms with a powerful near-death experience. If the NDE is positive and highly detailed, it will blow the person's worldview apart, as near-death experiences do not support either the doctrinal views of the religious person or the 'nothing's out there' views of the atheist. If the NDE is distressing, the religious person's literal worldview may survive, but there will be years of agonizing about the prospect of hell. The atheist, who has no context or vocabulary for such an event, will either scramble to piece together a new (often extreme) worldview or is likely to believe the experience was a psychotic episode.

Few people have anyone to point them to developmental stages as an instrument for understanding how these kinds of changes work. As a result, they and the people around them suffer. It may be an average agnostic or "none," or an ordinary Methodist or Muslim tormented by a shift from doctrinal faith into the questionings of stage 4, or it may be a bewildered spouse trying to understand why her previously religious husband has come back from his hospitalization as a near-death experiencer who thinks he is an atheist because his boundaries have shifted; she does not know where to turn for help. The problem is, people are left on their own to figure things out.

Surely we can do better!

NDES AND DEVELOPMENT

A few years ago, twenty-five near-death experiencers participated in a retreat sponsored by the International Association for Near-Death Studies, the first such event exclusively for experiencers. All but two had had a highly positive NDE.

For three days the group discussed the challenges they had faced since their NDE, their conclusions later reported in the *Journal of Near-Death Studies*. The article indicated decisively that on almost every line of development, the NDE had catapulted them precipitously from a conventional position and set of values into an abrupt and often uncomfortable new stage.

Every one of the retreat respondents reported feeling changed by the NDE: "I was in tremendous pain over the reality of restructuring my life." "I had to put the pieces of my life back together in a new way."

Keep in mind that the most common adult developmental level is Stage 3, with Stage 2 next in frequency. The universal message of the positive near-death experiences centered on the importance of unconditional love and how we treat each other—values belonging to Stages 5 and 6.

For the retreat experiencers, the result of the new outlooks was confusion and friction in almost all important areas of their lives: relationships, careers, money, religion. Views on social issues underwent major upheaval: attitudes towards violence, prejudice, disease, poverty, or justice. Political loyalties turned upside down. The changes often split relationships with friends and family.

Seventeen retreat participants had divorced since the NDE, thirteen of them saying their divorce was due in part to incompatibility over their changed values. "I wouldn't react the same; money no longer mattered," "My unconditional love for others was misinterpreted," "My attitudes and values all changed," "A position of power no longer meant anything to me," "I saw how my job was irrelevant," "I could no longer tolerate the avarice and greed."

Some participants belonged to places of worship in which they felt affirmed and were more spiritually nourished than ever before. Of those from more restrictive religious backgrounds (Stages 2-3), 78 percent had changed their views and no longer held to their church teachings of heaven, hell, God, evil, or sin. Such a radical change in views often left them alienated from family, friends, and their traditional religious community.

Most had changed careers. Of all the retreat respondents, 70 percent had become active in some type of healing work, with nine of these working fulltime as physicians, ministers, therapists, self-help writers, counselors, or related professionals. Five were involved in building or working in mind/body/spirit centers. Here, too, these service-oriented occupations reflect the post-conventional interests of stages 5 and 6.

Only two people in the group reported distressing NDEs; but one effect was shared even by those with the most glorious NDEs: the experiencers "retreated into isolation and depression, feeling as if they no longer fit in, like strangers in an alien world where few people understood or believed them."

Clearly, without a more gradual developmental gradient, the explosive nature of an NDE can produce cataclysmic social and personal trauma.

For those who would romanticize movement into the more highly nuanced stages of the post-conventional level, this may serve as a cautionary tale. Be warned: As the stage development literature says, the often isolated individual at level 5 "lives and acts between an untransformed world and a transforming vision and loyalties." It is worth remembering that at Stage 6, it is often these radically actualized people, the "subversives," who are done away with in the name of conformity and, like Martin Luther King, Jr., are honored as martyrs and have holiday Mondays named after them.

CHAPTER 18

Chimps, Bonobos,
and the Rest of Us

Genealogy fascinates just about everyone, especially when a really famous or interesting relative shows up. The June, 2012 issue of *Nature* magazine surely intrigued us all for its report that not only do we share almost 99% of our DNA with chimpanzees, our closest relatives, but now that is true also of bonobos, the chimps' sibling species. It seems that we swim in DNA pools which are 98.7% identical.

What I find most fascinating is the behavioral complexity of this news: We don't simply *look* similar, we also act similarly.

Chimpanzees are known to be aggressive, hostile toward strangers, power-hungry, often violent to the point of murderous. Male dominated, they are known to form attack gangs to roam their territory looking for outsiders to fight and kill. When stressed, a male will kill unprotected infants not his own. Put into the context of whatever the evening news is this week, the comparisons are likely to be painful.

On the opposite side of the Congo River, the chimps' siblings, the bonobos, are the only peaceful ape. They are cooperative with each other, curious rather than hostile toward outsiders, and alpha-female-dominated. Unlike chimps, bonobos share easily, even sharing food with strangers; they do not patrol the borders of their territory or practice infanticide.

It is not that bonobos do not experience conflict; they do. However, says Duke University researcher Brian Hare, bonobos will bite, but they won't kill. Primatologists say they are hyper-sexual, preferring to "make love not war" as a way of resolving conflicts. Whereas chimps tend to address conflict with violence, bonobos of both genders prefer to settle scores with non-procreative, sometimes homosexual, sex. Journalist Andrew Sullivan reports about one laboratory experiment that "at times the chimps were too busy fighting each other to complete tasks. But the sexually hyper-promiscuous bonobos could focus." How very intriguing.

And here, then, are we *homo sapiens*, sharing equally, it seems, not only all that DNA but the personality characteristics of *both* chimps and bonobos. No wonder life seems so demanding! Genetic inheritance being the ground on which—or perhaps with which—we build our human enterprise, it is those characteristics which get incorporated into our institutions, and therefore into our churches and banks and schools as well as our insurance agencies and kickball teams and mega-corporations. Oh, good gosh.

Knowing this background, it should come as no great surprise that across the millennia, as *homo sapiens* has wrestled with the questions that became religion, there should be a strain that has understood its ultimate authority, its god, as a controlling and often angry entity, power-ridden and hostile to outsiders, ready to punish those who do not submit to rules and the will of the leadership. Jealous, it will kill its children rather than share authority, and will go to war for the sake of increasing possession or pride.

Here is the judgmental aspect of human thought which stresses condemnation, whether expressed in social law or religious dogma. It is the chimpanzee aspect of our DNA which produces the attitudes of a wrathful God, whether in the Ancient Near East or the 21stcentury, and which conceives dogmatic theologies of hell as eternal physical torment in the name of a harsh justice.

This chimpanzee aspect of religion works. It has largely sustained Christianity for some thousands of years and provides structure and meaning to the lives of millions of worshippers around the world. As fear is the primary force one has been taught to experience, it seems natural. And yet, as the Christian writer John Shore puts it,

> 'Love me, because I love you. And if you don't love me, I'll torture you forever.' What would that be, from the Stalker line of Hallmark cards? What kind of sickness is that? And what kind of unhealthy relationship must it produce? Who wants to be in a relationship because they're too afraid not to be?

Why this matters is the point of a powerful statement by Frank Schaeffer, son of the famous evangelist Francis Schaeffer—and if you read nothing else on this subject, read the blog post from which this quote is taken, "There is No Hell: God Just Couldn't Be Meaner Than We Are." (If you don't have a computer, it's worth a trip to the library to read his brief post on one of theirs, or get a friend to print a copy for you; the link is in the bibliography.) He summarizes the implications of what I am perhaps unfairly calling "chimpanzee religion":

> So whether you're an atheist or not, the issue of who's going to Hell or not matters because there are a lot of folks on this planet – many of them extraordinarily well-armed – from born-again American military personnel to Muslim fanatics, who seriously believe that God smiles upon them when they send their enemies to Hell.

And so my view of "Hell" encompasses two things: First, the theological question about whether a land of eternal suffering exists as God's "great plan" for most of humanity.

Second, the question of the political implications of having a huge chunk of humanity believe in damnation for those who disagree with their theology, politics and culture, as if somehow simply killing one's enemies is not enough.

What most people don't know is that there's another thread running through both Christianity and Islam that is far more merciful than the fundamentalists' take on salvation, judgment and damnation.

It is with relief, then, that we can now claim our inner bonobo, which has been part of human history—and thus of Christianity and all human religion—all along. A harsh theology of punitive atonement is not the only valid approach wired into our potentials.

In human terms, the bonobo approach envisions purpose as loving, gracious, and compassionate. Its reality need not be trouble-free, but its religious expression conceives a creative force which manifests in building relationships of trust, not as lists of beliefs to be memorized or demands to be met, not as appeasements of an antagonistic deity, and not as borders between hostile camps.

Seen from this perspective, life and religion are no longer monuments to fear, a matter of protecting the self from threats by God or other authorities. Rather, when trouble comes, and conflict—as they will—they can be interpreted not as vengeance or punishment but as part of the fabric of life, to be dealt with through engagement in negotiating and reconciling, courage, compromise and trust. This attitude leads to a life freer from fear, whatever happens. To see the character of life's very existence as gracious, loving, and compassionate does not mean that bad things do not happen, but that we learn to deal with them without despair.

This stream of "bonobo faith" runs through all the major religious traditions, although they express it in different images; after all, we share this genetic heritage. In our Western, Abrahamic tradition, metaphors of the sovereignty of love and nurturing parallel those of violence and harsh justice: the thunder god, the blood-soaked warrior, the devil prowling 'like a hungry lion, seeking whom to devour' run right alongside shepherd, mother, father, lover, protecting eagle.

In other words, it is not the fault of religion itself that so many familiar doctrines are harsh and unloving; the fault is in the influence of the more violent strain of our nature. Religion will be whatever we make it. And although our power centers may look at this kinder approach with derision, genome sequencing has now demonstrated that the way of love and compassion can claim as much validity as any other. As Schaeffer says in his blog post, "Wasn't 9/11 enough of an argument against retributive religion?" The choice of where to place our trust has always been available; it is up to us to claim our own.

CHAPTER 19

NDE, Religion, and Buried Treasure

Be joyful though you have considered all the facts.

—WENDELL BERRY, *MANIFESTO*

This book is not religious.

Or maybe it is. Maybe my other book and the blog are too. Or maybe not.

I think of my writings as being perhaps religious in its widest sense but *non-doctrinal*—though to a great many people non-doctrinal means anti-religious. I think of the writings as being faith-filled. They are all about spirit (or Spirit) and numinous experiences and questions. A *numinous experience* is any event that feels like a contact with a transcendent reality, which to many people makes it feel religious. A deep near-death experience is one kind of numinous experience. I believe it is about faith, as described by James Fowler and other significant writers in the twentieth century.

"Questions of faith," wrote Fowler, "aim to help us get in touch with the dynamic, patterned process by which we find life meaningful. They aim to help us reflect on the centers of value and power that sustain our lives. The persons, causes and institutions we really love and trust, the images of good and evil, of possibility and probability to which we are committed—these form the pattern of our faith.

Faith is not always religious in its content or context... Faith is a person's or group's way of moving into the force field of life. It is our way of finding coherence in and giving meaning to the multiple forces and relations that make up our lives. Faith is a person's way of seeing him or herself in relation to others against a background of shared meaning and purpose. [Stages of Faith]

FAITH, NDE, AND RELIGION: LIKENESSES

Faith has to do with an unseen and often inexpressible aspect of life, something beyond the physical. So does near-death experience. Religion has to do with particular expressions of those aspects.

Faith has to do with values, relationships, self-discovery. So do NDEs. Religion has to do with specific ways of expressing them.

Faith has to do with an ancient and continuing sense of a mysterious, intelligent force greater and more meaningful than can be described. So do some NDEs. Religion tends to collect stories of encounters with that force, with specific explanations of its meaning.

Faith, or its observance, transforms a person's life. So do most NDEs. So can religion.

Faith has more to do with life on earth than it does with an afterlife. So, I believe, do NDEs, and religion. My view.

Most people seem to confuse faith with religion, as meaning some type of belief in a set of facts about the supernatural. It is not that. But what with one thing and another, we rarely have opportunity these days to discuss questions of faith. In this chapter, I am hoping to make a small dent in this mountain of need.

As I see it, there are two major differences: For one thing, an experience is felt individually, and faith is individual, while religion is lived in community. Second, over the past thirty years NDEs have received good press and been wildly popular with the public. Religion has not. Faith seems often to be considered quaint.

Why is this? It is clear that questions concerning religion lie behind many difficulties with understanding near-death experiences and all their close spiritual relatives, most especially the distressing ones. Here, for example, are two examples:

> "It's terrifying that such a god might exist and is actually believed to exist by millions and millions of people. I agree with the other poster who said they pray that religion isn't real: such a possibility is a nightmare."

> "I don't know what to believe any more, and I am so afraid. What is wrong with religion?"

When people find nothing but that to say about religion, it is for sure that we have fallen on hard times. This withering drought of understanding is brought about by bone ignorance, which is not usually the fault of the speakers of these unfortunate statements, but which they unwittingly perpetuate.

They certainly illustrate ignorance of "metonymy," the figure of speech in James Thurber's famous "the Container for the Thing Contained." You go to a restaurant and want soup. The waitress asks, "Cup or bowl?" You answer, "Cup, please." Now, you do not want a *cup;* you want the soup that will be *in* the cup. That's metonymy.

The women who made those two statements above are clearly mistaking the Container (religion) for the Thing Contained (a noisy bunch of anger-based interpretations which make up a mere slice of the whole of religion). They do not recognize that *religion* is a vast continent of which the 'religion' [sic] they are thinking about is but a tiny, shrunken peninsula of judgmentalism and fear, heavy on control and strong on punishment. That version is not 'religion' *per se* but has certainly mastered the marketing. The statements further illustrate the deplorable state of religious education in altogether too many places.

This climate of distaste and widespread unfamiliarity with personal religion makes discussing the relationship between religion and transcendent experiences extraordinarily difficult. Someone is always jumping up and stomping out of the room in disgust.

Some of the stompers are plain ignorant about religion. Based upon absolutely no exposure to what I mean by the term, they claim, usually stridently, that religion must be abolished. Considering religion's durability over the course of human history, this is about as sensible as saying that mathematics should be made illegal because so many of us have difficulty understanding it.

Some stompers have been so deeply wounded by the excesses of a particular religious establishment (there are many possibilities to choose from) that they want nothing to do with any mention of religion. It's hard to blame them.

Most other room-stompers are individuals whose identity is so fully engaged with a narrowly focused religious expression which they consider the *only acceptable one* that any other is considered quite probably evil. This is typically what happens when a tradition focuses on being 'right,' on believing that their facts are the only possible truth, and on punishing those who disagree. The tradition is likely to have been around long enough to gather a good deal of intellectual ornamentation (doctrines, rubrics, details of belief) to which their followers are required to attach.

EXPERIENCER, RELIGION, AND NDE

First, a definition: Spirituality can be pursued as an individual activity, but religion is by definition a group endeavor. At its broadest, by *religion* I mean an organized human response to the call of the sacred as revealed in a particular spiritual narrative with its images and symbols. That 'call of the sacred' seems to be wired into most of us, and 'religion' is merely a category of response—what happens when a group of people agree to respond to Spirit in relatively the same way and as an organization. There are thousands of ways, most of which will teach that they are the one *true* way. Like it or not, at least in quantity, religion is real. Whether what a particular religion teaches is factual (*that* sort of 'real') is a different question.

Religion, then, is a natural outcome of human wonder and curiosity about the universe and our place in it. Humans are social creatures who talk to each other, and share ideas, and gather with like-minded others around those ideas. Get rid of human questions and sharing of ideas, and religion will disappear. "I'm spiritual but not religious" has been gathering adherents long enough that it is already showing signs of doctrine, the shared convictions which are an early stage of becoming a religion.

With a single exception—Hinduism, which goes back too far to see its beginnings—every one of the world's enduring religions began with the numinous experiences of a single individual: Confucius (Confucianism), Lao-Tzu (Taoism), Moses (Judaism), Jesus (Christianity), Siddhartha Gautama (Buddhism), Mohammed (Islam). One could add Joseph Smith (Church of Latter Day Saints) and the founders of any number of cults. Their teachings about the meaning of human existence and how the universe works—or a narrative about them—attract followers, who find ways of gathering and then ordering themselves and the teachings, and they become the foundation of an organization. A religion.

Religion, then, like NDEs, comes to us by way of *experiencers* who tell others what they have learned. Patterns of thinking emerge, which well-meaning *non-experiencer* followers develop and organize into principles about the material. The non-experiencers inevitably fail to "get it" completely, no matter how many words, narratives, rituals, logical arguments, or symbols they use in the attempt to capture what the founder has described. The same is true of NDEs and efforts to understand *them*.

Non-experiencers may not fully grasp the transcendent quality of their subject, but they are the ones who, in the early days of a religion, will teach the newcomers and children, draft a creed, hammer out doctrines and organizational policies. With NDEs and other spiritual events they will be the early authors, the television producers and workshop leaders, the researchers and journalists and interviewers who tell audiences how to interpret what they have heard. Bit by bit, the meaning of their explanations shifts more toward material explanations they understand, as the intuitive basis of the original is taken over by logical analysis. Surprisingly quickly, the dynamics of human ego come into play and soon saturate the organizational effort—all the clutter of power, control, influence, greed, fear, self-importance, anger, political maneuvering—threatening to distort and pervert the original insights. It's unavoidable. This is not negativity talking, or cynicism; it's the empirical data of a long lifetime in organizations. It is knowing the story of the two of Jesus' disciples who wondered if they would sit next to him in heaven. Whining does not help. A smile and good psychology will.

DISTRESSING DOCTRINE AS METAPHOR

All spiritual talk consists of human attempts to communicate the indescribable, which is of course impossible. The closest approach, and the one we fall into most naturally, is by way of the language of metaphor and myth, which are able to point towards subjects too big for words alone.

Where the rubber meets the numinous road, so to speak, is where the essentially metaphoric nature of spiritual experience meets the expectations of the literal-minded material and organizational world. All spiritual talk is interactive, an interplay between the ordinary and the transcendent, flesh and blood people and spirit.

The "real world" hears experiences and translates them into a physical reality of factual happenings which can be understood as literally true. Thus, spiritual and religious experiences and NDE accounts and the experiencers' interpretations are heard as if they were videotaped, journalistic reporting of the highest factuality. Religious talk of hell and eternal punishment leads to terrifying expectations of what may happen in a physical (or quasi-physical) sense when we die. However, this is a great misunderstanding of how spiritual language works.

John Sanford (1970, 22) says simply, "Conscious minds think conceptually; the unconscious expresses itself in symbol." Lionel Corbett (1996, 45) says, "The simplest way in which the Totality makes itself known to the ego is by means of an image." Edward Edinger (1972, 209) makes the important observation that a symbol is "an image or representation which points to something essentially unknown, a mystery."

The late, great theologian Walter Wink's monumental work *The Powers That Be* is a study of "powers and principalities" as personifications of such ideas as hell, greed, and evil. He gives this vivid portrait:

> The new age dawning may not 'believe in' angels and demons the way an earlier period believed in them. But these Powers may be granted a happier fate: to be understood as symbolic of the 'withinness' of institutions, structures, and systems. People may never again regard them as quasi-material beings flapping around in the sky, but perhaps they will come to see them as the actual spirituality of actual entities in the real world. (1986, 172-173)

Note that Wink does not claim that the forces formerly thought to be physical angels and demons do not exist; as forces, they can be real and powerful. However, he and a host of other writers have demonstrated that the forces are no longer to be thought of as external to us but are resident in our very unconscious. Yes, there is unpleasantness in the spiritual realms, and we must own it along with the peace and rapture, just as we must own our Shadow along with our God-loved Self. It is not the fault of *religion* nor of *numinous experiences* that this is so, but the fault of every one of us who is too willing to follow the opinion of an authority rather than do the difficult work of study and thinking for ourselves to see what holds true and what must be reworked.

By now, you will recognize that the issue is really the developmental stage of the speaker. Those demanding only the literal level will grasp it from the perspective of Stages 2 or 3. Those saying, "But there's more!" are at least at Stage 4; they recognize that even the deepest of beliefs shift and change with human experience.

This is not news. As early as the fourth century C.E., the British monk and theologian Pelagius, (c. 354-418), wrote in one of his letters:

> You will realize that doctrines are inventions of the human mind, as it tried to penetrate the mystery of God. You will realize that Scripture itself is the work of human minds, recording the example and teaching of Jesus. Thus it is not what you believe that matters; it is how you respond with your heart and your actions. (*The Letters of Pelagius*, quoted by J. Philip Newell, *Listening for the Heartbeat of God: A Celtic Spirituality*. Paulist Press: 1997, 11-12).

THE METAPHORIC LIFE

Here is my favorite story about religion:

In the midst of a desert of rock and sand and not much else, there was a spring of pure water. An oasis grew around the spring, where tall trees offered shade, and the air was full of the scent of flowering plants and fruits, and birds and small animals ran in the undergrowth.

Caravans discovered the oasis as a powerful place of rest and refreshment. The air was cooler than on the baking desert, and the life-saving water was sweet and cold. One traveler was so grateful that he placed a small rock beside the spring as a tribute. Other grateful visitors did the same.

Soon the spring was surrounded by a ring of stones. After a while the ring became a low wall, on which visitors rested. As more and more stones were added, travelers could no longer reach the water, though they could still see it. And then the spring was entirely hidden, with only the sound of water as a reminder of what had once been there. But still visitors came and told stories about the place.

Eventually, the stones made such a great mound that even the sound of the spring was hidden. Yet travelers continued to come bringing their tribute stones because they had heard the story of a life-giving spring that had once been in that place. Others considered the notion of such a spring a foolish, made-up tale, the wishful thinking of people who could not accept the reality of a harsh and waterless desert.

Deep below the hot sand and the rocks and tributes, clear, cool water ran in the dark, as it had since the Beginning.

As above, so below; as with religion, so with NDEs. For anyone struggling with the mountain of religious doctrinal notions about human nature, guilt, judgment, punishment, hell, and eternal torment, let me suggest that the challenge involves recognizing the difference between rocks and the treasure they obscure. In Western culture, as in others, the natural spring consists of two simple statements:

Love [the sacred] with all your heart and strength and mind
Love others as you do yourself.
Everything else is tribute stones.

[Ed: The story of the oasis I owe to theologian and educator Louis M. Savary, PhD, S.T.D., who, with his wife, psychologist Patricia H. Berne, PhD, teachers extraordinaire, taught me at least half of everything I know.]

CHAPTER 20

NDE, Religion, and the Limit of Our Sight

Writing about distressing near-death and other spiritual experiences has been the mental equivalent of training for a triathlon. You have no idea! Because the subject matter is both so personal and so experimental, *everything* has to be examined: "Do I really mean this?" "What does it mean to say [that]?" "How true is it that...?" "Who knows about...[subject requiring a decade of study]?" The challenges go on and on.

And so it occurs to me that I must have lost my mind to undertake a topic like religion and near-death experience, especially distressing NDEs with so many connotations reaching in so many directions. WordPress, which hosts the blog, reports that what I write there is being regularly read in 146 different countries. Readers range from "I-know-I've-been-there" experiencers, to religious believers alarmed by the absence of doctrinal confirmation, to intrigued mainliners (that's the religious mainline, not the drugs kind), and a wide range of "other" faiths. There are scornful religiously dismissive atheists, confused atheists, atheists homesick for community, and the wavering, spiritual-but-not-religious Nones. There is also a smattering of people who wandered in by mistake and seem to be staying until their perplexity abates. How to speak to all those perspectives...especially as mine may be altogether different? And yet, the exercise seems to work.

What I am trying to do, you see, is to get down underneath all the preconceptions and assumptions, all the theories and doctrines, and ask, "What is bedrock?" Is it possible to get beyond overlays of supposition to something so simple I am able to trust it? Can we begin to see near-death experiences through lenses other than doctrinal or disbelieving or medical? As you surely recognize by now, I don't *have* answers. All that's possible is to share with you my questioning and tentative conclusions, recognizing that we can barely see to the end of our own skin. The meaning of the universe may well be elsewhere; I offer merely a weathervane.

"Life is eternal, and love is immortal, and death is only an horizon; and an horizon is nothing save the limit of our sight." (Rossiter W. Raymond)

I have loved this quote since I was barely a teen, although of those four clauses, there's only one of them I trust absolutely. (At least it's a start.). You can see that my engagement, shall we say, with the weekly Bible group at church is different than most (yes, every Wednesday morning, in the parish hall at St. Philip's).

Last week, this doctrinally heterogeneous group was intently debating whether the creeds have any credibility for today, dating as they do from around the year 323. And one man, a charming and orderly minded retiree, said he relied on the creeds to give him a sense of structure in the world.

"There's so much confusion," he said, "how could I know what sense to make of it without the creeds?"

And that's when it struck me that in a universe where so very many of our questions and fears are unanswerable, doctrine and creeds are like grab bars in the shower—something to hold onto so we don't fall. It doesn't matter whether or not they're provable or genuinely part of the underlying structure; they're at least cognitive architectural features offering stability when we're a bit off balance. Some of us need more of them than others do.

All our descriptive systems—theologies, ideologies, party platforms, disciplines, paradigms—are grab bars of one sort or another, ways of ordering information to help us find our way around this vastly mysterious universe without falling into a chaos of disordered observations. Models. Maps. Architectures. And we all like to believe that ours is The Right One, the one most surely anchored to The Way Things Are. At least, we say, our own makes sense, unlike those others!

Over at the *Paranormalia* blog, host Robert McLuhan points to an article in which the writer says of her avowedly atheistic system of confirmed skepticism, "I'm part of a growing community (some would even call it a movement) consisting of hundreds of thousands of people worldwide who value science and critical thinking... I felt we were doing important work: making a better, more rational world and protecting people from being taken advantage of." (I assume you will notice the assumption of superiority in there, the air of colonialism.)

In that writer's "better, more rational world," people are protected from anything religious because she considers it an intellectual scam. Meanwhile, at the extreme other end of the scale, as our blog's commenter Philemon points out, reviews of Eben Alexander's *Proof of Heaven* have included "attacks on the book [for] not according with Christian doctrine, and one goes so far as to call it a trick by Satan to lead Christians astray."

We do persist in clutching our own treasured beliefs as being The Way Things Are.

And here's where the trouble begins. By simply stating this observation, suggesting that perhaps we can't quite discern which is the *only* Truth or that there may be no *only* to truth, I kick at the foundations of somebody's grab bars, the supports which make that person's life feel secure.

If our systems, our grab bars, are all models, if they are maps rather than actuality, if there can be more than one set of supports, how can we know which one is true? And if none is uniquely True—especially if *mine* is not ultimate Truth Forever—how can I believe anything? Do all supports fall? Am I safe?

This, I think, is the hairsbreadth pivot on which everything turns. The greatest challenge of near-death experiences: that they force ordinary people to confront new and huge and scary truths about being alive and conscious. Heavenly or terrible, they are like a command to grow up, to mature on the spot, to take a wider view than we are ready for. There is more to reality than what we believe when we are small, and more than can be articulated by any single mind or any single human belief system. Can we accept that?

Mystical experiences are a threat only to those who cannot bring themselves to accept the true size of the universe, the true breadth of Truth. Faith systems, whether scientific or religious, work best in the world when they *suggest* rather than insist on restricting, when they cease demanding total control, when they allow for growth and exploration…in short, when they stop insisting that they are the god they would worship. We are being carried into new places and forced to examine everything we ever thought we believed.

How we answer to this challenge, it seems to me, will determine everything else about the way we think and live. How we answer will define the very essence of faith, and sanity, and quite possibly the future of the world. Stay tuned.

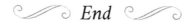 *End*

ACKNOWLEDGMENTS

In 2015, WordPress told me, the blog *dancingpastthedark* was read by more than 36,000 people in 146 countries. At least one person in Istanbul reads it, and a handful of people in Iran and Saudi Arabia and South Africa, and more in Germany and Russia and Brazil, and in 140 other countries around the globe. I wish it were possible to thank each one personally.

I constantly thank my daughter Katy Evans-Bush, a writer in London, for insisting that I start the blog which is the origin of this book.

With the first book, *Dancing Past the Dark,* a person known to me only as RabbitDawg swept in out of Internet-land and, more sheep dog than his moniker, began herding me around the online field. He showed me how it worked, introduced me around, promoted the book before and after it was published, and has kept insisting there was another book to be written. We have met only online. I couldn't have done this without him. RabbitDawg, Henry Brand, there aren't enough thank you's!

Steve Volk, journalist and author of *Fringeology*, wrote a review so stunningly perfect that even I could believe a second book would be a workable venture.

Robert McLuhan, who treated the material as if it were actually normal, and who welcomed me in, has been a wonderfully stabilizing force.

Thank you to the beta readers of this book, my Wednesday morning group who took time out from Bible-study-with-a-difference to read and comment and improve what's here. Tom and Karen Griffin, Dick and Jenny Lee, Ruth Posey, Stan Shelton, Bill and Harriet Wheeler—every author needs such enthusiasm and clear-eyed support! Stan himself demonstrates that when you need an editor, look for a literate engineer.

And always, deepest thanks to Nancy Poe Fleming for endless encouragement, support, re-readings, suggestions, and supper on the table. Making all things possible, all the time.

ABOUT THE AUTHOR

Nancy Evans Bush, MA, was hired in 1982 as office manager, soon to be executive director, of the fledgling International Association for Near-Death Studies (IANDS), of which she is now a past president. She has been a consistent voice for the substantial minority of near-death experiencers whose NDEs feature fear, despair, guilt, and even terror rather than heavenly realms. A long-time editor of the IANDS magazine *Vital Signs* and author of numerous articles for the *Journal of Near-Death Studies* and other publications, she also wrote the first study of children's near-death experiences. Her books are *Dancing Past the Dark: Distressing Near-Death Experiences* and *The Buddha in Hell and Other Alarms: Distressing Near-Death Experience in Perspective.*

Before her involvement with near-death studies, she taught secondary school English, was a grant writer and research associate for one of the first pediatric nurse practitioner programs in the U.S. (at the University of Connecticut), was director of an urban employment and training program for the U.S. Department of Labor, and became a freelance technical writer. Her degrees are a BA in English from SUNY at Albany and a Masters in Pastoral Ministry and Spirituality from St. Joseph University in Connecticut. Now semi-retired, she lives in coastal North Carolina, USA, where in good weather she can be found gardening or trying a new restaurant. She is the mother of three adult children, with seven grandchildren and one great-grandchild.

You can read Amy Stringer's interview with her at David Sunfellow's always-interesting site, *New Heaven New Earth:* http://ndestories.org/wp-content/uploads/2012/04/VS_Reprint_NEB_ Fall_2009.pdf

OTHER BOOKS
BY THIS AUTHOR

"Absolutely enthralling—literary, adventurous, incisive, informative and smart... one of the strongest, most thought-provoking books on the paranormal I've ever seen."

—STEVE VOLK, JOURNALIST AND AUTHOR.

"Dancing Past the Dark is what we have all been waiting for. [a] thoughtfully deep and inspiring response to the question of meaning... masterful - a must for any experiencer of a near-death state (no matter what kind) or a spiritual transformation."

—P. M. H. ATWATER, NDE RESEARCHER AND AUTHOR

"...an outstanding piece of work...a wonderfully comprehensive and rich history of what can be known and what might be considered about NDEs. The book bursts with anecdote and commentary, reinforcing for the reader that there is always another way to see things."

—WAYNE ROLLINS, MDIV, PHD, THEOLOGIAN
AND JUNGIAN SCHOLAR, AUTHOR

"A valuable contribution to the NDE literature and engagingly written. It needs to be seen and read by the wider public."

—J. HAROLD ELLENS, PHD, COLONEL, U.S. ARMY (RET.),
CHAPLAIN, PSYCHOTHERAPIST AND AUTHOR:

"I love, love, love, love this book!"

—MADELAINE LAWRENCE, RN, PHD, UNIVERSITY
OF NORTH CAROLINA, WILMINGTON, NURSING
EDUCATOR AND RESEARCHER, AUTHOR

CONNECT WITH NANCY EVANS BUSH

I really appreciate your reading this book!

Follow me (occasionally) on Twitter:
http://twitter.com/nancyevansbush

Subscribe to my blog:
http://www.dancingpastthedark.com

Visit my website:
http://www.dancingpastthedark.com

Contact me (often a longish wait):
nanbush12 at gmail dot com

BIBLIOGRAPHY

Aquinas, Thomas. Summa Theologica, Third Part, Supplement, Question XCIV, "Of the Relations of the Saints Towards the Damned," First Article, "Whether the Blessed in Heaven Will See the Sufferings of the Damned?" Amazon Digital Services. 2012.

Athet Pyan Shinthaw Paulu. Buddha in Hell. *http://amightywind.com/ whatsnew/ 071112buddhist.htm*

Babinski, Edward T. "Christians Debunk Resurrection of Buddhist Monk in Myanmar (Burma)" *http://etb-pseudoscience.blogspot.com/2012/04/ christians-debunk-resurrection-of.html*. Retrieved May 1, 2012.

Bailey, Lee W. A "Little Death": The Near-Death Experience and Tibetan Delogs. *Journal of Near-Death Studies* 19(3), 2001.

Bekov, Marc and Jessica Pierce. *Wild Justice: The Moral Lives of Animals.* Chicago, IL:University of Chicago Press. 2009.

Bell, Rob. *Love Wins.* New York: Harper One. 2011.

Borg, Marcus J. *Speaking Christian: Why Christian Words Have Lost Their Meaning and Power—And How They Can Be Restored* (Kindle Locations 1138-1143). New York: Harper Collins, Inc. Kindle Edition. 2011.

Bush, Nancy Evans. *Dancing Past the Dark.* Cleveland, TN: Parson's Porch Books, 2012.

Campbell, Joseph. *The Inner Reaches of Outer Space: Metaphor as Myth and as Religion, 55, 1986.* New York: Harper & Row.

Carey, Frances . *The Apocalypse and the Shape of Things to Come.* Toronto:University of Toronto Press. 1999.

Carlson, R. "Demon.". Retrieved from *http://theophiliacs. com/2008/09/14/demons/* November 3, 2008.

Corbett, Lionel. *Psyche and the Sacred: Spirituality beyond Religion.* New Orleans: Spring Journal, 2007.

Croner, Barbara and Sheila Joshi. "The Descent Experience & the Tertium Non Datur: Managing the tension and the time of waiting". *http://neuroscienceandpsi.blogspot.com/2013/01/the-descent-experience-and-tertium-non.html* Retrieved January 10, 2013.

Dawson, Samuel G. "The Rich Man, Lazarus, & the Afterlife." *http://www.truthaccordingtoscripture.com/documents/death/the-rich-man-and-lazarus-dawson.php*

Dietrich, R.F. "A History & Criticism of 'The Apocalypse.' *Rennes-le-Château website http://chuma.cas.usf.edu/~dietrich/apocalypse.html Retrieved February 9, 2011.*

DiLeo, Francesco B. "Nadir Experiences in the Process of Transcendence," *The Journal of Religion and Psychical Research,* October, 1985.

Edinger, Edward F. *Ego and Archetype.* Baltimore, MD: Pelican, 1974.

Enns, Peter. The Bible Tells Me So: Why Defending Scripture Has Made Us Unable to Read It. New York: HarperCollins: 2014.

Evans, Rachel Held. *Searching for Sunday.* Nashville, TN: Thomas Nelson. 2015.

Ferwerda, Julie. *Raising Hell: Christianity's Most Controversial Doctrine Put Under Fire.* Publisher: Author. 2011.

Fowler, James W. Stages *of Faith: The Psychology of Human Development and the Quest for* Meaning. New York: Harper & Row. 1981

Gallup, George Jr. and William Proctor. *Adventures in Immortality.* New York: McGraw Hill. 1982.

Gibbs, John C. *Moral Development & Reality.* Thousand Oaks, CA: Sage. 2003.

Grayden, John J. *Near-Death Experiences in Hell.* ITBD International. 2014.

Greenspan, Miriam. *Healing through the Dark Emotions: The Wisdom of Grief, Fear, and Despair.* Boston, MA: Shambhala. 2004.

Greer, John Michael, . *Apocalypse Not: Everything You Know about 2012, Nostradamus and the Rapture is Wrong.* Berkeley, CA: Viva Editions. 2011.

Greyson, Bruce and Nancy Evans Bush. "Distressing Near-Death Experiences," *Psychiatry,* Vol 55, February 1992.

Grof, Stanislav and Christina Grof. *Beyond Death: The Gates of Consciousness.* New York Thames and Hudson, 1980.

Grof, Stanislav and Christina Grof. *Spiritual Emergency: When Personal Transformation Becomes a Crisis.* Los Angeles: Tarcher. 1979.

Grof, Stanislav. *The Holotropic Mind.* San Francisco: HarperCollins. 1992.

Grof, Stanislav. "Psychology of the Future: Lessons from Modern Consciousness Research," *http://www.stanislavgrof.com/wp-content/ uploads/pdf/ Psychology_of_the_Future_Stan_Grof_long.pdf*

Grof, Stanislav. *Realms of the Human Unconscious.* New York: Dutton. 1975.

Haule, John Ryan. *Perils of the Soul: Ancient Wisdom and the New Age.* York, ME: Weiser. 1999

Hell *http://www.angelfire.com/fl4/Biblestudy/misc/ HELL.html*

Jung, C.G, transl. R.F.C. Hull. *Psychology and Western Religion.* Princeton, NJ: Princeton University Press: Bollingen Series. 1984.

Kelsey, Morton T. *Afterlife: The Other Side of Dying.* New York: Crossroad: 1982.

Lao Tsu, Stephen Mitchell, transl. *Tao Te Ching.* New York: Harper Perennial, Compact Ed., 1992.

Lukeman, Alex. Book review of Edward F. Edinger, *Encounter with the Self.* Retrieved from *Tiger's Nest Review.* Created 3/25/98; accessed 9/4/01. *http://www.friii.com/~tigrnest/encount.htm*

Lukeman, Alex. *Nightmares: How to Make Sense of Your Darkest Dreams.* New York: M. Evans, 2000.

Lukeman, Alex. *Dreams from the Other Side.* M. Evans. 2002.

Malarkey, Kevin. *The Boy Who Came Back from Heaven.* Carol Stream, IL: Tyndale House, 2010.

McLaren, Brian. *A New Kind of Christianity.* New York: HarperCollins. 2010.

Moody, Raymond. *Life After Life.* St. Simon's Island, GA: Mockingbird Books. 1975.

Newberg, Andrew. *Why God Won't Go Away: Brain Science and the Biology of Belief,* Ballantine Books. 2008.

Newell, J. Philip. *Listening for the Heartbeat of God: A Celtic Spirituality.* Paulist Press: 1997, 11-12.

Perriman, Andrew. *http://www.postost.net/lexicon/hell-unbiblical-doctrine/ /* Retrieved January 2012.

Perriman, Andrew. *Hell and Heaven in Narrative Perspective.* CreateSpace. 2012

Perry, John Weir. *Trials of the Visionary Mind.* Albany, NY: SUNY Press. 1998.

Perry, Robert. "The Realness of NDEs." *http://www.monkeywah.typepad.com\paranormalia* 2011\10\the-realness-of-ndes.html Retrieved October 2011.

Rawlings, Maurice. *Beyond Death's Door.* Nashville, TN: Thomas Nelson. 1978.

Rawlings, Maurice.. *Before Death Comes.* Nashville, TN: Thomas Nelson. 1980.

Rawlings, Maurice.. *To Hell and Back: Life After Death—Startling New Evidence.* Nashville, TN: Thomas Nelson. 1993.

Rohr, Richard. This talk, originally titled "How Jesus Interpreted Scripture," was presented via webcast in December 2013. *Hierarchy of Truths: Jesus' Use of Scripture* CD. Albuquerque, NM: Center for Action and Contemplation, 2013.

Rommer, Barbara. *Blessing in Disguise.* Llewellyn Publications. 2000

Sabom, Michael B., MD. Review of *Beyond Death's Door,* by Maurice Rawlings, MD. *Anabiosis,* 1(3). 1979

Sabom, Michael B., MD. Review of *To Hell and Back: Life After Death—Startling New Evidence,* by Maurice S. Rawlings. *Journal of Near-Death Studies,* 14(3). 1996.

Sanford, John A. *The Kingdom Within*. Paulist Press. 1970.

Schaeffer, Frank,. "There is No Hell: God Just Couldn't Be Meaner Than We Are." Patheos blog, December 12, 2012. *http://www. patheos.com/blogs/frankschaeffer/2012/12/there-is-no-hell-god-just-couldnt-be-meaner-than-we-are/#sthash.UqrQwiyC.dpuf*

Shore, John. "Is Hell Real? What Are We, Six?" Patheos blog, *May 24, 2011, http://www.patheos.com/blogs/johnshore/2011/05/ is-hell-real-what-are-we-six/*

Shore, John. *Hell No! Extinguishing Christian Hellfire* (Kindle Locations 37-39). Kindle Edition. 2011.

Stout, Yolaine., Jaquin, L., Atwater, P.M.H.. "Six major challenges faced by near-death experiencers," *Journal of Near-Death Studies* 25:1, Fall 2006, 49-62.

Swedenborg, Emmanuel, *Heaven and Hell: The Portable New Century Edition*. Bryn Athyn, PA: Swedenborg Foundation. 2010.

Tart, Charles T. *States of Consciousness*. E.P.Dutton. 1972.

Tedeschi, Richard G, Chrystal L. Park, and Lawrence G. Calhoun, (Eds.). *Posttraumatic Growth: Positive Changes in the Aftermath of Crisis*. Lawrence Erlbaum Associates. 1998.

Turner, Alice K, *A History of Hell*. New York: Harcourt Brace. 1993.

Zaleski, Carol. *Otherworld Journeys*, New York: Oxford University Press. 1987.

INDEX

Edinger, Edward, 171
ego, 51, 100, 170
Einstein, Albert, 15
Elliott, Ann K., 129–30, 132, 137, 140
Enoch, Book of, 59–60
extraordinary human experience
    (EHE), 22

fairness, children's sense of, 97
faith
    and growth/exploration, 178
    and NDEs, 165–68
    stages of, 151–55
fears about life goals, 125–28
Ferwerder, Julie: *Raising Hell*, 87–88
fire, 13, 58, 75
First Nation peoples, 149
First Sight, 137
Fowler, James: *Stages of Faith*, 151,
    165–66
Francis, Pope, 26
Freud, Sigmund, 109

Gallardo, Camilo, 133
Gehenna (near Jerusalem)
    association with suffering and
        destruction, 65–66
    as hell, 73–74, 77
    mentioned by Jesus, 63, 64, 65, 66
    New Testament on, 85
Geller, Uri, 44
genealogy, 159
Genesis, Book of, 118
genetic inheritance, 160
God
    contrast created by, 118
    as criminally abusive, 76–77
    and fallen angels, 60, 74

as fire, 13
Kingdom of, 61, 62, 63, 66
as loving, 69–70
reward/punishment by, 57
as wrathful, 69–70, 73, 160–62
good vs. evil, 58–59
Gospels, 62–65
Greek religions (ancient), 60, 74
Greenspan, Miriam, 51
Greyson, Bruce, 23
Grof, Christina: *Beyond Death*, 110–12
Grof, Stanislav, 136
    Beyond Death, 110–12
    "Psychology of the Future," 106–9

Hades (king of the Underworld),
    114–15
Hades (Underworld), 56, 60–61, 64,
    73–74. *See also* hell
Hammurabi code, 46, 97
Hare, Brian, 160
Haule, John Ryan, 8
Heaven and Hell (Swedenborg),
    89–90
Hegel, Georg Wilhelm Friedrich,
    118–19
hell, 55–143. *See also* afterlife;
    Buddha in hell; Hades; Sheol;
    Tartarus
    Abominable Fancy, 70
    ancient development of the
        concept (before Jesus), 57–60
    Augustine on, 72, 74, 76
    Book of Enoch on, 59–60
    cognitive dissonance of, 76
    Dante on, 72–73
    doctrinal/traditional, 14, 17, 27, 32
    and doctrinal vocabulary, 74–76

emotional force of, 32
as eternal physical torment, 66, 73, 75–78, 160–61
and Evangelicals, 86–87, 92–93
fear of, 85–86
Gehenna as, 65–66
Gospels on, 62–68
as incommensurate justice, 76–77
individual's psyche as source of, 78–79
lake of fire in, 68–69
as a material place, 78
as punishment after death, 32
Rawlings on, 91–95
reality of, 81–83
Revelation on, 68–70
Swedenborg on, 89–90
vocabulary of, 74–76
as the "worm that does not die," 66–68
"Hell: Origins of an Idea," 86
Hick, John, 76
Hillenbrand, Candy, 128, 129
Hinduism, 169
Hittite code of laws, 57
Holecek, Andrew, 121–22
Holloway, Gillian, 125–28
holograms, 133
holotropic states of consciousness, 106–9
Honoré, Carl, 123

Inanna (Ishtar), 114
individuation, 128, 131
Inquisition, 71, 73
interconnectedness, 111
International Association for Near-Death Studies, 156

irreconcilable conflict/dialectic of opposites, 117–19, 133, 150
Isaiah, 67
Israel (ancient), 61–62, 63, 66

Jeremiah, 65–66
Jerusalem, destruction of, 63, 66
Jesus of Nazareth, 169
crucifixion of, 61–62
divinity of, 71
Gospels on, 62–68
as Messiah, 62
Paul's writings on, 62
teachings of, 61–62, 70
thieves crucified with, 132
Jewish community. *See also* Judaism
Greek influence on Jewish thought, 60–61, 62
rich vs. poor Jews, 61
story of poor man vs. rich man, 64–65
Job, 46, 116
John, Gospel of, 63, 65
John of Patmos, 68
Joshi, Sheila: "The Descent Experience and the Tertium non datur," 113–14
Journal of Near-Death Studies, 156–57
Judaism
on Adam and Eve, 72
Book of Enoch, 59–60
Torah, 97–98
Jung, Carl G., 89, 111
on the axiom of Maria, 142
on crucifixion experiences, 130
descent experiences of, 115–16
on individuation, 128
on mental opposites, 119, 120, 125, 132–34

CPSIA information can be obtained
at www.ICGtesting.com
Printed in the USA
BVHW042047161221
624206BV00012B/1039

9 780985 191719